Warwick Illustrated Encyclopedia

SCIENCE

Warwick Illustrated Encyclopedia

SCIENCE

Brenda Walpole

WARWICK PRESS
New York/London/Toronto/Sydney

Published in 1989 by Warwick Press,
387 Park Avenue South, New York,
New York 10016.

First published in 1988 by
Grisewood & Dempsey Ltd., London.

Copyright © Grisewood & Dempsey
1988.

Printed in Spain
Library of Congress Catalog
Card No. 88-51102
ISBN 0-531-19050-1

Contents

Introduction

Science is a way of investigating the air, water, earth, atmosphere, and all the living things around us by careful observation and experiment. Wherever you go in the world, science is a vital part of the life of each and every person. The great store of scientific knowledge that we have today has been built up over many centuries. The pioneers of science were all people who had ideas and couldn't wait to try them out. Great discoveries have been made by amateurs with improvised equipment as well as by those working in highly sophisticated laboratories. Early scientists studied everything from anatomy to physics and chemistry, but today many scientists specialize in just one branch of science.

So far, our observations and experiments have led us from the invention of the wheel to a computer-controlled landing on the moon. Stories such as that of Newton "discovering" gravity when an apple fell on his head, may or may not be true. What *is* true is that we are interested in the things that happen around us and that science has no limits—there is always something new to discover.

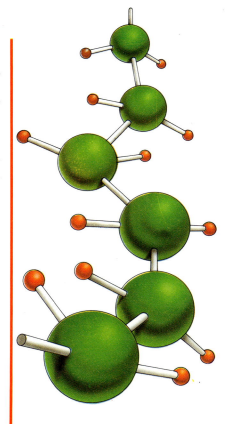

BRANCHES OF SCIENCE

Science	Study of
EARTH SCIENCES	
Geology	Rocks, earthquakes, volcanoes, and fossils
Meteorology	The atmosphere and weather
Mineralogy	Minerals, their location and mining
Oceanography	Waves, tides, currents, trenches, and ocean life
Paleontology	Plant and animal fossils
Petrology	Formation and structure of rocks; their chemical content

LIFE SCIENCES

Agronomy	Land management of crops and cultivation
Anatomy	Structure, form, and arrangement of the body
Bacteriology	Bacteria, their growth and behavior
Biology	Animals and plants; origin, morphology, and environment
Botany	The plant world
Cytology	Structure, function, and life of cells
Ecology	Relationship between living things and environment
Medicine	Cause, prevention, and cure of disease
Nutrition	Supply of adequate and correct foods to satisfy the body's requirements
Pharmacology	Drugs; their preparation, use and effects
Physiology	The function of living things
Psychology	Behavior of humans and animals; working of the brain
Zoology	Animals

MATHEMATICAL SCIENCES

Logic	Reasoning by mathematics; used by computers
Mathematics	The application of geometry, algebra, and arithmetic etc.; application of these to concrete data
Statistics	Numerical information which is to be analyzed

PHYSICAL SCIENCES

Aerodynamics	The properties and forces of flowing air on solid objects
Astronomy	Heavenly bodies and their motions
Chemistry	Properties and behavior of substances
Electronics	Behavior of electrons in a vacuum, in gases, and in semiconductors
Engineering	Application of scientific principles to industry
Mechanics	The invention and construction of machines, their operation, and the calculation of their efficiency
Metallurgy	The working of metals; smelting and refining
Physics	Nature and behavior of matter and energy

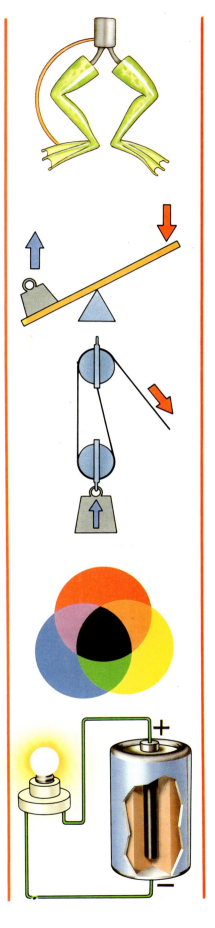

1. Water, Water, Everywhere

We drink it, we wash in it, we swim in it—water is all around us. It has no taste, no smell, no color, and yet it is the world's most useful substance. Without it there would be no life on earth. Our own bodies are 70 percent water and water is vital to every plant and animal.

To a visitor from outer space, earth would appear a very unusual planet. It is unique in two important ways: it is the only planet in our solar system to have living things on it and it is the only one with liquid water—lots of it. The oceans cover seven-tenths of the earth's surface. We have all this water because our planet is just the right size and just the right distance from the sun. Because of its size, earth has enough **gravity** to prevent tiny drops of water vapor drifting off into space. And it is not so close to the sun that the water is boiled away as steam, but not so far away that it becomes frozen solid.

Water is actually one of the commonest minerals, and is the only one found naturally in a liquid form.

Around and around the water goes

If you put a dish of water in a sunny place, it will soon

About four billion years ago, the earth was a red-hot ball with tiny drops of water in its atmosphere. Any water that touched its surface turned to steam. Then the earth cooled, pools of water collected and rain fell for years, until most of the earth was covered in ocean.

THE WATER TABLE

There is water known as "ground water" underground, beneath the earth's surface. This water seeps through the surface from rain, rivers, and lakes. It is stored in porous or permeable rock (rock that can absorb water). The level to which the rock is totally full of water—saturated— is called the water table. Ground water sometimes occurs naturally as a spring, or it collects in wells drilled down through the porous rock.

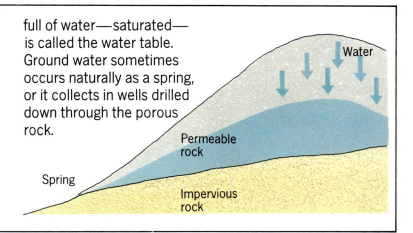

Water

Permeable rock

Spring

Impervious rock

Water evaporates

begin to dry up. But where has the water gone? It has not simply disappeared, it has been taken up into the air as tiny droplets called water vapor. We call this process **evaporation**. Water evaporates all the time from the surface of seas, rivers, and lakes. It rises into the air and forms clouds in the sky. As the clouds cool, bigger drops of water form again and these fall as rain, hail, or snow. After a while, this water finds its way back into the seas, rivers, and lakes; so the water around the earth is never lost. The total amount of earth's water is about the same as it was over four billion years ago.

Above: The earth's "water cycle." Heat from the sun makes water in rivers, lakes, oceans, and on the land evaporate and rise into the air as water vapor. High in the sky, the air is cold and cannot hold the vapor, which condenses to form the drops of water that make up clouds. Eventually this water falls back to the ground as rain.

Putting water to work

Have you ever stood by a big waterfall and heard the roar as it thunders down? Water is heavy. Falling water is very powerful and if we can control its power it can do useful work for us. People have used water power for thousands of years. The ancient Egyptians used water wheels turned by flowing rivers to turn mill stones for grinding grain. Today, new kinds of water wheel are used to drive big generators that make electricity. We call this "hydro-electric power."

Some hydroelectric power comes from natural water-falls such as Niagara Falls, but more often artificial falls are made by building dams. A dam is a huge, thick wall built across a river to stop its flow. Water builds up behind the dam wall to form a deep lake. The greater the distance the water must fall from the dam, the more power it can produce when it is released. Some of the water is chan-neled down through big pipes. The pipes shoot the falling water against the blades of a water wheel called a "turbine." The turbine's blades are rather like ships' propellers. These blades spin large generators to make electricity.

Hydroelectric power makes only a small part of the world's electricity. Most of it is made by burning coal or oil. But hydroelectric power does have its advantages. Where there is a suitable river, it is cheap to produce and pollution-free. And, when our coal and oil supplies have run out, water will still be with us in abundance.

Falling water is immensely powerful, as we can see from waterfalls like those shown in the photograph below, the Iguassu falls in Brazil.

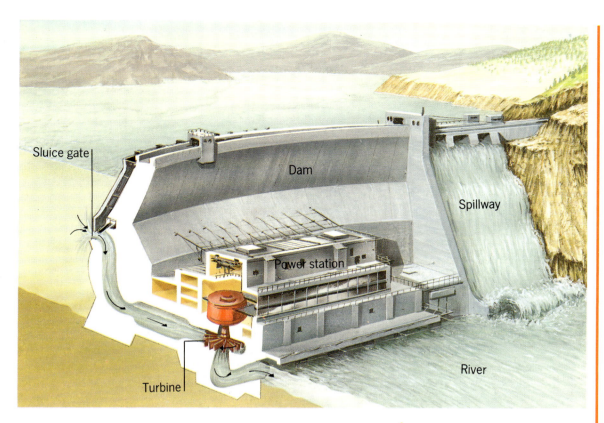

Tides and waves

There are other ways of using the power of water. In the river Rance in France the water rises more than 30 feet when the tide comes in. A low-level dam or barrage was built right across the river. As the tide comes in, water rises over the dam. When the tide falls again, the dam holds back the water until there is enough difference in height to turn 24 turbines that make electricity.

The flow of water from the lake through this hydro-electric power station's turbines is controlled by the sluice gates. When the turbines are not working, water can flow down to the river along the spillway.

POWERFUL TURBINES

Modern water turbines spin at high speed. They are among the most powerful machines in the world. The turbine shown here is called a Francis turbine. Most of the world's biggest hydroelectric plants use this kind of machine. Water under great pressure rushes in to spin the blades. The blades turn the shaft which spins the electric generator and an electric current flows.

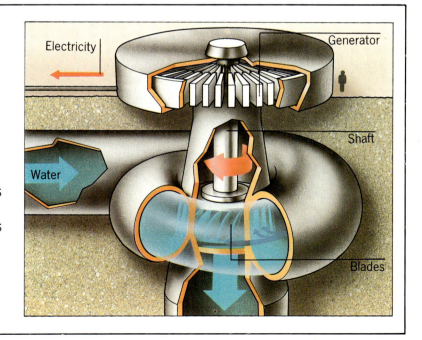

Other inventors have tried to use the energy of the waves that pound on the world's seashores. They have anchored rows of floats or rafts which bob up and down in the waves. This bobbing motion works generators to make electricity. But so far no one has made a very successful wave machine. Wave machines really work on the power of the wind. It is winds which stir up the sea to produce waves.

Floating and sinking

Why do some things float and others sink? Why does a small metal nail sink, while a huge metal ship floats? Floating has nothing to do with weight. It all depends on **density**.

Density is the amount of **mass** (matter) something contains. Imagine two objects, both the same size but made of different materials—a brick and a block of wood, for example. The brick will sink in water but the block of wood will float. The brick is much denser than the wood.

The density of a substance is given in grams per cubic centimeter—the number of grams a cubic centimeter of the substance weighs. One cubic centimeter (cc) of water

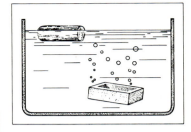

The piece of wood above can float because its density is less than that of water. A brick, of the same size, is more dense than water and so it sinks.

Below: *A submarine's density is low when its "ballast" tanks are kept full of air and so it can float. If water is pumped into the tanks to replace the air, the vessel's density increases and it dives. To resurface, air is pumped into the tanks to replace the water.*

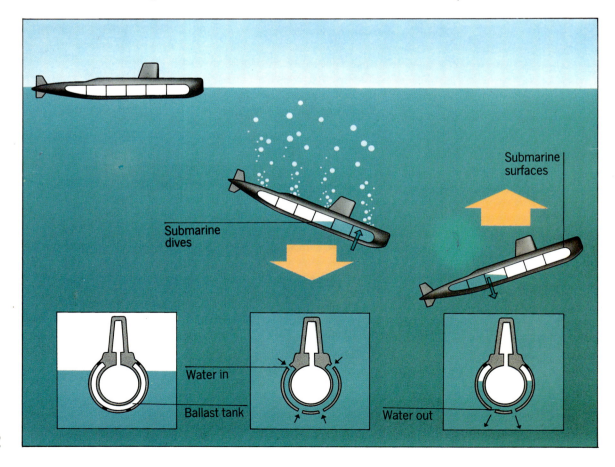

Submarine dives

Submarine surfaces

Water in

Ballast tank

Water out

weighs 1 gram, so the density of water is 1. Only things that have a lower density than water can float in water. One cc of lead weighs 11.3 grams. The density of lead is therefore 11.3, so lead can never float on water.

The story of Archimedes

Archimedes was a famous Greek scientist who lived about 250 B.C. The best-known story about him tells how he had the idea of finding the volume of an object by putting it in water. (Volume is the space taken up by something.)

King Heiron had a new gold crown. But he suspected that the goldsmith who made it had cheated him and mixed some cheaper metal with the gold. Heiron asked Archimedes to find out if the crown was pure gold.

Archimedes decided that if the crown was not pure gold, then a piece of pure gold that weighed the same as the crown would not have the same volume. But how was he to find the volume of an odd shape like a crown?

The story goes that the answer came to him as he stepped into a bath filled to the brim with water. Suddenly he realized that the water that spilled over onto the floor would have the same volume as his body. If he put the crown into a vessel full to the brim and caught the water spilled over, the spilled water would have the same volume as the crown. Archimedes was so excited by his discovery that he rushed naked into the street shouting, "*Eureka!*" (meaning "I've found it!").

When the great man did put the crown in water, it displaced more water than a piece of pure gold that weighed the same. So Archimedes was able to tell the king that the crown contained a lighter metal as well as the gold.

Archimedes is said to have had the inspiration to solve the problem of King Heiron's crown in the bath. But in the true tradition of science, he tested his theory by careful observations and experiments.

A strange substance

To us water seems a very ordinary substance because we are so used to it. But to the scientist it is one of the most interesting and unusual substances there is. One of the unexpected things water can do is absorb (soak up) enormous amounts of heat. More heat is needed to warm up water than is needed to raise the temperature of almost any other substance. This makes water very useful in cooling systems. It is used to keep things cool in cars and in nuclear power stations. Water in the radiator of a car absorbs heat from the engine and keeps it cool. But the water's own temperature does not rise very much.

When water is cooled, another unusual thing happens. At a temperature of 32°F (0°C) water freezes and turns into solid ice. As the water freezes, it expands (grows bigger). Most other things shrink as they freeze. Unfortunately for us, this means that if water freezes inside a pipe, it can burst the pipe as it expands.

Because water expands as it freezes, it becomes less dense—one cubic inch of water takes up a little more space when it becomes ice. Ice cubes have a lower density than water and this means that they can float. Next time you have a drink with ice in it, see how much ice is above the liquid. When sailors sight an iceberg they see only the part above the water. There is eight times more iceberg under the surface.

Ships traveling in arctic waters like this one, are often in danger from icebergs. Ice is slightly lighter than water so it floats—but only just. A good deal of the iceberg remains concealed below the surface.

The "steam" from a boiling pot forms as water vapor escapes from the hot water inside and meets the cooler air outside.

14

The power of steam

Warming ice turns it back into water. If we go on heating water, after a while it boils and turns into tiny droplets of vapor called steam. This happens at a temperature of 212°F (100°C). Steam needs lots of space. It expands to take up about 1,700 times more space than the water that made it. This means that it has great pushing power. You may have seen a small amount of steam lifting the lid of a pot of boiling water. The power of steam can be made to work for us. For more than a hundred years steam has pushed the pistons of engines which drive pumps, factory machines, and locomotives.

One of the first machines driven by steam was invented by an ironmonger called Newcomen in the early 18th century. It was first used in the Cornish tin mines to pump them free of water, although its use rapidly spread through Europe.

The steam engine, invented in the 1700s gave rise to the railways' golden "age of steam."

INSIDE A STEAM ENGINE

In a steam engine, the pressure of expanding steam is used to push a "piston" to and fro in a hollow tube called a "cylinder." The piston is attached to a rod called the "piston rod." As the piston rod goes out and in it drives another rod called the "driving rod." It is the driving rod that turns a wheel called the "flywheel." The flywheel evens out the movements of the driving rod. It goes on turning steadily even when the piston is at the end of a stroke and is not pushing. In a steam locomotive, the driving rod is attached to a driving wheel.

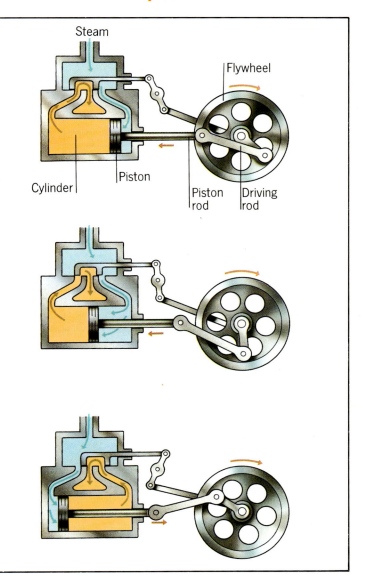

15

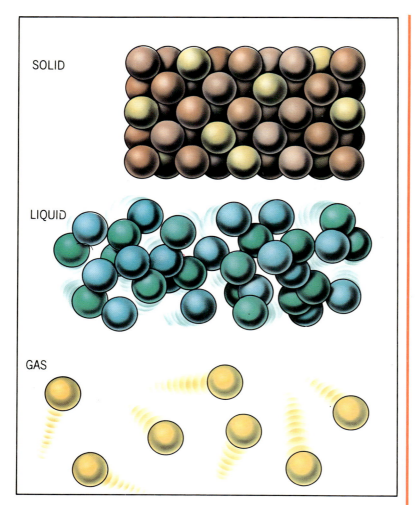

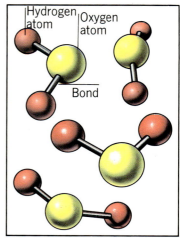

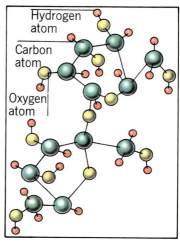

Solids, liquids and gases

Next time you see a kettle of water boiling, watch the steam rising from it. Heating water turns it from a liquid into a gas called steam. However, the "steam" that we say we see is not really the gas—it is a cloud of tiny water droplets called water vapor. The true steam gas forms immediately above the kettle spout. About an inch above the spout, this gas meets colder air and **condenses** into water vapor. If the water vapor meets a cold surface, such as a window pane, it turns into even larger drops of water. Frozen water, in the form of ice cubes from your refrigerator, will melt slowly in your favorite drink and turn back into water because the temperature outside the refrigerator is much warmer. Although they seem so different, steam, water, and ice are simply three forms of the same substance—one a gas, one a liquid, and one a solid. These are called "the three states of matter."

Above left: *Everything on earth is either a solid, a liquid, or a gas. Solids have molecules that are packed tightly together in regular patterns. Firm bonds hold them in place. Liquids have weaker bonds that allow molecules to move a little. But gases have no shape because their molecules can move around freely.*
Above top: *Each of these four water molecules has one oxygen atom bonded to two hydrogen atoms.*
Above bottom: *A sugar molecule contains 22 hydrogen atoms, 11 oxygen atoms, and 12 carbon atoms, bonded together to give it a unique shape.*

Here you can see two different forms of carbon: the graphite used in pencils and a diamond. Graphite has its atoms arranged in layers, and this makes it soft. A diamond has a complicated arrangement of atoms that makes it very hard and transparent.

The building blocks of matter

Just one tiny drop of water contains about 10,000 million, million, million even smaller parts called **molecules**. Steam, water, and ice all have the same kind of molecules. Each molecule of water is made up of still tinier parts called **atoms**. An atom is about one 250-millionth of an inch across. A water molecule has two atoms of hydrogen and one atom of oxygen. This is why scientists give water the shorthand name H_2O. Substances differ from one another because their molecules contain different kinds and numbers of atoms. As we saw on page 16, sugar is made of atoms of carbon, hydrogen, and oxygen. Substances which contain more than one kind of atom are called **compounds**. Sugar and water are both compounds.

Elements are substances that are made of just one kind of atom. For example, the element gold contains only gold atoms in each of its molecules. Gold, silver, and lead are examples of solid elements. Elements such as oxygen, hydrogen, and chlorine are gases, and mercury is a liquid. Just as heating ice turns it into water without altering its molecules, solid, liquid or gas elements can be changed in form. If liquid mercury is heated enough, it turns into a gas. If it is cooled a great deal, it turns into a solid. Heating the solid turns it back into a liquid again. All these forms of mercury contain exactly the same molecules. There are less than 100 natural elements and everything in the known universe is made of one or more elements.

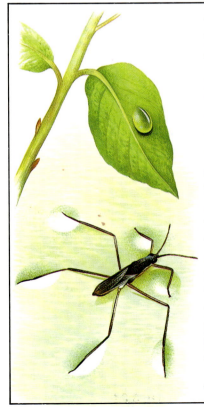

SURFACE TENSION—WATER'S STRETCHY SKIN

Have you ever wondered why the drops of water that drip from a tap, or the raindrops which rest on a leaf are round? Water forms round drops because of "surface tension." A molecule in the middle of a drop of water is surrounded by other molecules which all pull on it from different directions so that it stays in about the same place. But a molecule at the edge of the drop only has other molecules on one side of it so it is pulled more strongly toward them. Molecules on the surface of water are pulled inward and held closely together. This produces a force called surface tension which makes water behave as though it had a stretchy skin across its surface. You can float small objects such as pins on this "skin" and only dent it because surface tension supports them. Certain insects, such as pond skaters (shown on the left), can walk on water without sinking in. They stretch out their long legs to spread their weight evenly over the surface "skin."

Oxygen – the "O" of H_2O

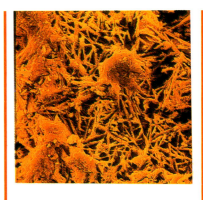

This photograph, taken through an electron microscope, shows rust on a car body. Small patches of rust flake off and leave fresh metal exposed to oxidation. Metal can be protected from rusting by a layer of paint or grease.

Oxygen is the most plentiful element on earth. In each molecule of water, one oxygen atom is joined with two hydrogen atoms. Nearly half the weight of everything in and on the earth is oxygen, including two thirds of your body weight. Pure oxygen is a colorless gas—it makes up about 20 percent of the air we breathe, but it joins easily with many other elements to form compounds called "oxides" in a process called **oxidation**.

Sometimes oxidation is very slow. Rust—scientific name "iron oxide"—is formed gradually as iron or steel combines with oxygen in damp air. Other oxidations are faster and more spectacular. When oxygen joins rapidly with other elements, **combustion** takes place—flames, light, and heat are produced. As a match is struck, friction against the match head begins the oxidation of chemicals in the head by oxygen in the air. There is a small explosion and the head bursts into flames, setting fire to the wood.

ROCKETS

Fuel in most engines burns in oxygen from the air, but rockets, which travel in space where there is no air, need to carry their own supply of oxygen as well as fuel. This oxygen is carried as LOX—frozen liquid oxygen. The fuel for rockets is usually liquid hydrogen.

The fuel is burned in a combustion chamber and hot gases pouring out at the bottom of the rocket push it along. Rockets that carry satellites into orbit have several stages, each carrying its own fuel. When the fuel in one stage is used up, it falls away.

The Saturn rocket which sent men to the moon had kerosene as its first stage fuel.

Firework rockets are propelled upward by burning gunpowder. In the front part of the rocket are packages of chemicals that produce the colored lights and bangs.

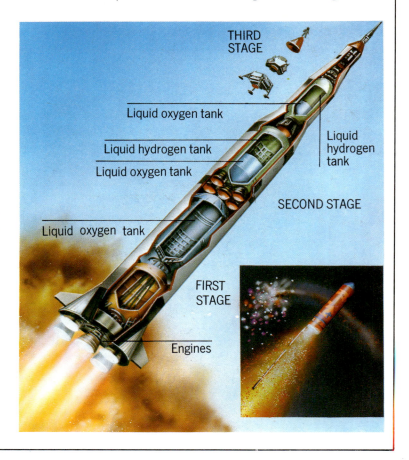

THIRD STAGE

Liquid oxygen tank

Liquid hydrogen tank

Liquid oxygen tank

Liquid hydrogen tank

SECOND STAGE

Liquid oxygen tank

FIRST STAGE

Engines

Hydrogen – the "H" of H_2O

Hydrogen is the lightest substance we know. About 90 percent of all matter in the universe is hydrogen. Although hydrogen makes up only one percent of earth's air, beyond our planet there is more hydrogen than anything else.

Most of the hydrogen on earth is found, combined with oxygen, in water, but combined with other atoms it forms part of many other vital substances. All acids (see page 82) contain hydrogen and so do important fuels such as methane (natural gas), gasoline and oil, which contain only hydrogen and carbon atoms.

We can separate the hydrogen from the oxygen in water by passing an electric current through it in a process called **electrolysis** (see page 61). In the early days of flight, hydrogen was used to fill balloons because it is much lighter than air and it allowed the balloons to rise. In 1785 Blanchard and Jefferies made the first flight across the English Channel in a hydrogen-filled balloon. But filling balloons and airships with hydrogen has led to problems. Hydrogen burns very easily when it is mixed with air. In 1937 a luxury German airship, the *Hindenburg*, exploded as it came in to land after a transatlantic flight, killing 36 people. A simple spark probably caused the explosion. Today, helium is used to fill balloons and airships. It is almost as light as hydrogen but it does not burn. Liquid hydrogen, made by compressing hydrogen gas, is used as a fuel, not to propel balloons, but to propel rockets into space.

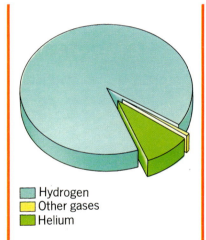

- Hydrogen
- Other gases
- Helium

The pie diagram immediately above shows the proportions of the various gases found in the universe. Some scientists believe that everything in the universe— the stars, our sun and the planets—were all made from hydrogen when the universe was first formed. Modern airships, like the one in the photograph at the top of this page, are filled with helium. They are used mainly for short city sightseeing trips. Passengers are carried in safety and comfort in a cabin underneath.

2. The Air We Breathe

Our earth is unlike any other planet we know because it has lots of water and is enclosed in a precious wrapping of air. Without air and water, nothing could live on earth. We need to breathe the oxygen in air to stay alive. Although we cannot see, smell, or taste air, we know it is there. We can feel the wind blow and watch it fill the sails of boats.

The air that surrounds the earth is called the **atmosphere**. It is a few hundred miles thick and is held down by the pull of the earth's gravity. Over three-fourths of all the air is concentrated in the "troposphere"—the layer of atmosphere that is closest to earth and is only about 10 miles thick. The troposphere also holds water in the form of vapor, rain, clouds, and snow. Our "weather" is the

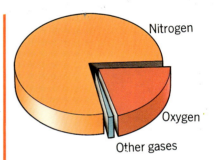

Above: *This pie chart shows the proportions of gases in the earth's atmosphere.*

WIND POWER

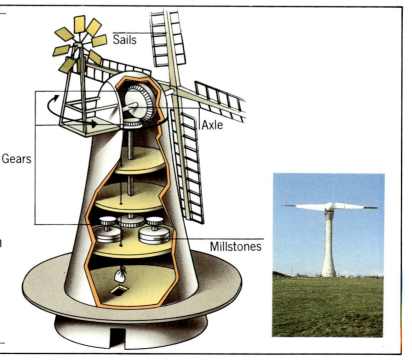

Windmills have been used to capture the power of the wind for more than 1,000 years. Traditional windmills like the one shown here were used to grind grain. The sails were attached to an axle which turned the mill stones that ground the grain.

The modern "windmill" in the photograph generates electricity for 1,000 homes in the Orkneys, Scotland. The two blades measure 200 feet from tip to tip.

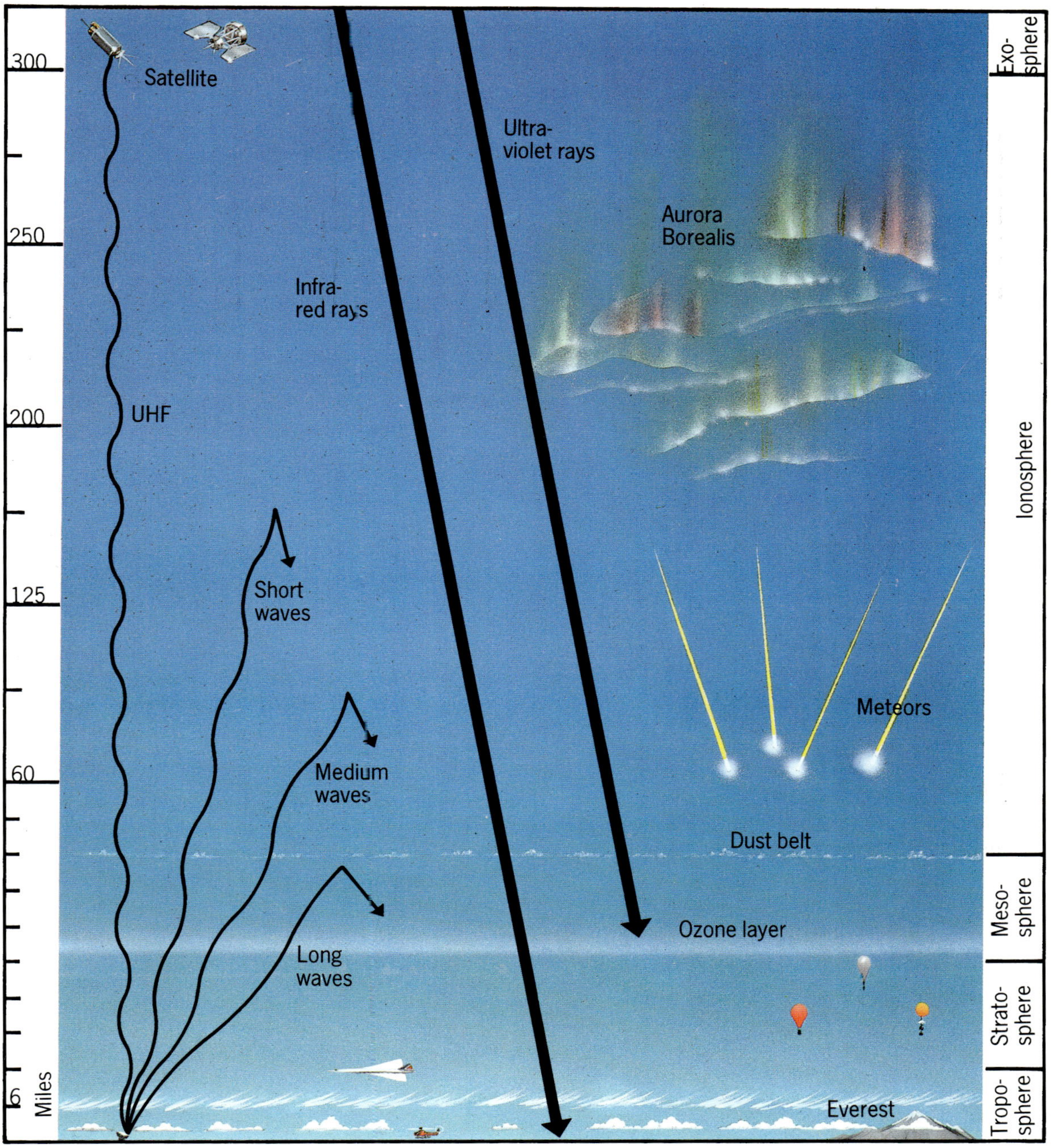
300
250
200
125
60
6
Miles
Satellite
UHF
Ultra-
violet rays
Infra-
red rays
Aurora
Borealis
Short
waves
Medium
waves
Long
waves
Meteors
Dust belt
Ozone layer
Everest
Exo-
sphere
Ionosphere
Meso-
sphere
Strato-
sphere
Tropo-
sphere

result of changing conditions in the troposphere. If people travel higher than this, to the top of mountains or in high-flying aircraft, they must carry a supply of oxygen or be enclosed in air-conditioned cabins which supply the oxygen they need.

As well as giving us oxygen to breathe, the atmosphere does other important jobs. It shields us from most of the sun's harmful rays. It also acts as a layer of insulation, keeping the temperature at levels which are neither too hot nor too cold for us to survive. Our moon has no air. Because of this, it has a temperature of 250°F during the day—much hotter than boiling water—and icy temperatures 280°F below freezing point at night.

Above: *The layers of the earth's atmosphere. The* troposphere *varies in thickness from 5 miles at the poles to 10 miles at the equator. In the* stratosphere *there is a layer of "ozone" that shields us from the dangerous rays of the sun. Above this protective layer, the temperature rises sharply in the thin, cloudless air.*

The pushing power of air

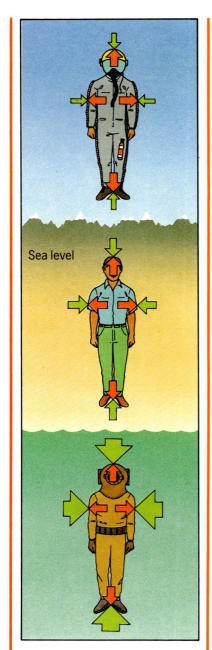

Although people may talk about things being as light as air, air is really quite heavy. One cubic yard of air weighs about a kilogram, more than the weight of this book. This means that at sea level, a column of air weighing about a ton is pressing down on each of us. We don't feel squashed by this huge weight because air presses in all directions, so the load—about 15 pounds for every square inch of our skin—is spread out all over our body surface. Also, the pressure of the liquids and air inside our bodies is about the same as the outside air pressure. Because under normal conditions these opposing pressures are balanced, we normally feel no discomfort.

Air pressure—the pushing force of the air—varies at different places on earth. As you climb higher, way above

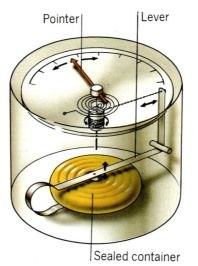

Pointer | Lever

Sealed container

An aneroid barometer (left) consists of a sealed metal container with thin walls. It has no air inside and its sides are held apart by a spring. As air pressure outside increases or decreases, the sides are pushed closer together or move farther apart. The movement of the container moves a lever, which in turn moves a pointer around the marked scale on the face of the barometer.

At high altitude, air pressure is low and there is not enough oxygen to breathe. Jet pilots wear breathing apparatus connected to an oxygen supply. At sea level, air pressure is balanced by the pressure from inside the body. Far below the sea, divers must wear suits to protect them from the great pressure of water above them. They also carry oxygen.

sea level, the atmosphere is thinner and air pressure becomes lower. Because the pressure from inside a person's body stays the same, traveling to a place where the air pressure is lower can be very uncomfortable, as pressure starts to push outward from inside the body. There is also less air to breathe and this can cause dizziness in people not used to high altitudes. Aircraft have pressurized cabins which keep the pressure the same as it is on the ground, so that passengers can breathe easily and feel comfortable. Below the sea, divers experience not only the pressure of air, but also of the water above them and the deeper they go the greater the pressure. To protect their bodies, they travel in submarines or wear pressurized suits and helmets.

Sea level

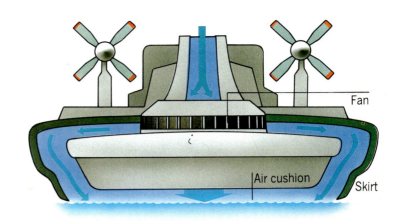

Fan

Air cushion

Skirt

An air cushion vehicle floats on a supporting cushion of air, provided by the large flat fan which blows air underneath it. The flexible rubber "skirt" helps to keep the air in. A craft 20 feet in diameter hovers about 2 feet above the ground.

Hovercraft are driven by propellers or jets and steered by rudders.

The main advantage of these craft is that they can be used to cross rivers or the sea and ride over rough or swampy land where other vehicles cannot travel. In such situations they give a relatively smooth ride, because of the cushion of air.

Air pressure varies from place to place as well as at different heights above or below sea level. When air is warmed it becomes lighter and rises. This means that air pressure tends to be lower over hot areas of the earth, such as deserts. Cold, heavy air sinks down, giving greater pressure in regions such as the Arctic and Antarctic. This sinking, cold air spreads outward, producing cold winds which blow toward warmer, low-pressure areas. Winds carry clouds and rain with them, so information about air pressure can help in weather forecasting. Atmospheric pressure is measured by instruments called barometers. Rising air pressure over a number of days usually means that the weather is going to improve.

AMAZING AIR

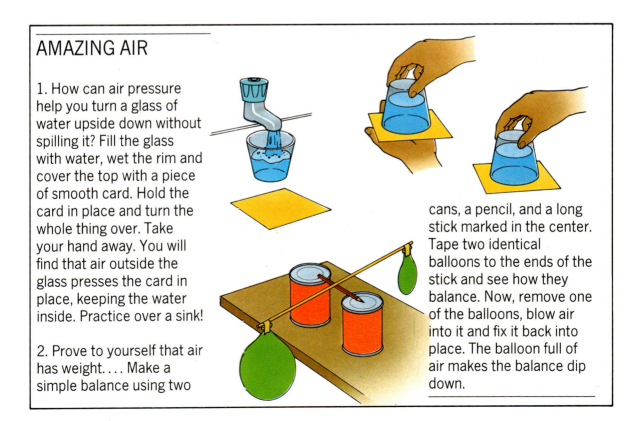

1. How can air pressure help you turn a glass of water upside down without spilling it? Fill the glass with water, wet the rim and cover the top with a piece of smooth card. Hold the card in place and turn the whole thing over. Take your hand away. You will find that air outside the glass presses the card in place, keeping the water inside. Practice over a sink!

2. Prove to yourself that air has weight.... Make a simple balance using two cans, a pencil, and a long stick marked in the center. Tape two identical balloons to the ends of the stick and see how they balance. Now, remove one of the balloons, blow air into it and fix it back into place. The balloon full of air makes the balance dip down.

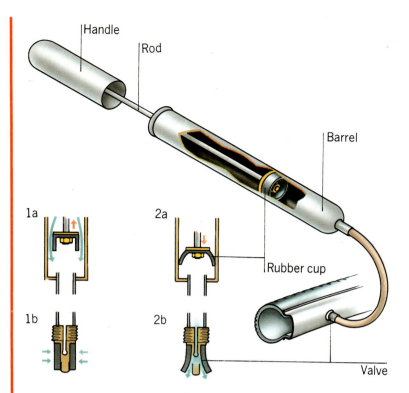

Handle

Rod

Barrel

1a

2a

Rubber cup

1b

2b

Valve

The bicycle pump shown here has a long rod with a handle at one end and a rubber cup at the other. The barrel is attached to the tire by a short tube. As the rod is pulled up, air is sucked into the barrel (1a) and the tire valve remains closed (1b). When the handle is pushed down, the air is compressed. This air pushes the sides of the rubber cup against the barrel so that no air can go back past the cup (2a). The air pressure inside the pump is now greater than inside the tire, so the tire's valve is forced open, letting air rush into the tire (2b).

Compressed air and vacuums

A good way to see how air behaves as it fills up a space is to pump air into a bicycle tire. As you pump, you squeeze or "compress" more and more air into the tire. The more you pump, the harder it becomes to continue pumping because more and more air molecules are being squeezed into the limited space of the tire. The compressed air in a bicycle tire, kept inside by a valve, can support the weight of both you and your bicycle. Even larger tires full of air can hold up a huge, ten-ton truck. When a "pneumatic" tire (a tire filled with air), hits a bump in the road surface, the air temporarily becomes further compressed. As this compression occurs, the shock of the bump is absorbed. As we saw on page 23 with the air cushion vehicle, air forms a cushioning, light-weight filling enabling things to float easily. If air is compressed, it fills many other useful objects, such as dinghies and life jackets.

Blow a balloon up and release it without tying the neck and you will see how powerful the escaping stream of air is as it shoots the balloon away from you. If it is controlled, a release of compressed air can be useful. Steady streams of high-pressure air, which can be produced by machines called compressors, drive pneumatic drills or road hammers, capable of breaking through solids such as concrete.

A pneumatic road drill contains a piston that is forced downward by compressed air. The piston drives the blade down with such force that it can break through concrete.

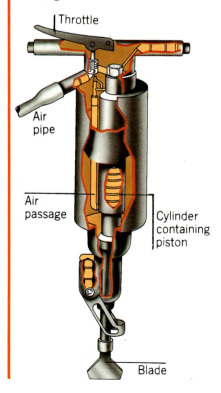

Throttle

Air pipe

Air passage

Cylinder containing piston

Blade

Empty spaces

Squashing air into an enclosed space increases its pressure, but if we suck air out of a space, the effect is the opposite. We can see this if we use a suction cup to fix something to the wall. Pressing on the plastic sucker forces air out from inside it. Because there is less air now underneath the sucker, the pressure there decreases. The sucker is held firmly in place by the greater pressure of air pressing against the outside of it. As you drink through a straw you reduce air pressure by sucking air out of the straw. The greater pressure of the air pressing down pushes the liquid up the straw into your mouth.

Many foods, such as bacon, coffee, cheese, and peanuts are sealed in packets which have had the air drawn out of them to keep the food fresh. The packets may be marked "vacuum packed" and they usually look flat because the greater air pressure outside presses them inward. A true **vacuum** is an empty space with no air, or anything else, inside it. In fact, perfect vacuums are impossible to make. Even solid containers give off tiny amounts of vapor. Vacuums are curious spaces. Neither heat nor sound can travel easily across them because there are too few molecules to transmit heat or sound energy. Vacuum flasks can keep a drink hot or cold because they have two walls which are separated by a vacuum. Heat from a hot drink cannot escape from the inner container to the outer wall of the flask. Similarly, heat from outside cannot get into the inner container to warm up a cold drink. Hot drinks do cool down eventually.

If a ringing alarm clock is put inside a large sealed jar, and the jar is connected to a pump, the sound of alarm becomes fainter as the air is gradually pumped out. Sound cannot travel through airless space because there are no air molecules to carry the sound waves.

To pump

BALLOON IN A BOTTLE

You can inflate a balloon by creating a partial vacuum.
1. Heat the air inside a bottle by standing it in a bowl of warm water for a few minutes. The air expands as it is warmed and so the pressure inside the bottle increases.
2. Fit a balloon over the neck of the bottle. Then stand the bottle in a bowl of cold water.
3. As the air inside the bottle and balloon cools, its pressure drops. The greater pressure of the outside air pushes the balloon into the bottle and inflates it.

1

2

3

3. The Science of Sound

Sounds travel in waves that push through things and spread out from the source of a noise, rather like ripples on a pond when a stone is dropped in. We hear sounds when the waves reach our ears. Sound waves don't just travel through air, they also move through other materials such as brick, stone, glass, and water.

Producing sound

To find out how a sound begins, twang a stretched rubber band and watch as it vibrates. The vibrations compress air molecules next to the rubber band, which in turn temporarily compress air molecules next to them. This "knock

Below: *Sound waves spread out from the tuning fork when it is struck. The outer part of our ears is specially shaped to collect sound waves and channel them inward, to the ear drum. As the ear drum begins to vibrate, it sends messages along the auditory nerve to our brain and we can hear the sound.*

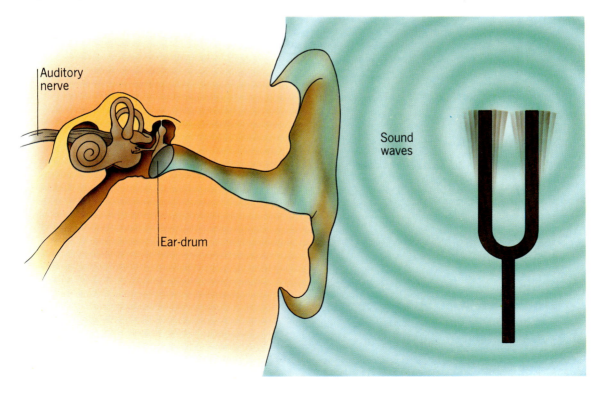

Auditory nerve

Ear-drum

Sound waves

on" effect produces traveling sound waves. Farther from the rubber band the effect decreases and the sound becomes fainter. A tightly stretched rubber band vibrates rapidly, and so the sound that you hear is high-**pitched**. Because the waves of vibration follow each other very frequently, we say that high-pitched sounds have a high **frequency**. A slack rubber band vibrates more slowly. It produces low frequency, deeper sounds which have more spread-out waves. Frequency is the number of waves passing a fixed point every second. It is measured in units called **hertz**. One hertz is equal to one complete wave —cycle—per second. The volume of sound—how loud it is—depends on how much energy the vibrations pass on

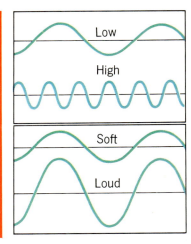

Above: *Sound waves can be shown like this on an instrument called an oscilloscope. High pitched sounds have waves that are close together. Low pitched sounds have longer waves. Loud sounds make the highest waves.*
Left: *Your brain can sort one sound from another and make it more or less prominent.* Below: *A powerful organ produces sounds that can be "felt" as they reverberate through a building.*

through the air. A very loud sound makes more intense waves than a softer sound. Sound waves can be shown as a wavy line on a special instrument called an oscilloscope —loud sounds make higher waves than softer ones. The height of the waves shown on the oscilloscope is called the **amplitude** of the sound.

Sounds like music

Hitting two pot lids together makes a din which is a mixture of sounds of many frequencies. Musical instruments make much more pleasant sounds by playing notes of just one or two frequencies. Groups of musicians often use specially made "tuning forks" to make sure that they all play the same note at the same pitch or "in tune." Tuning forks are made of metal which, when struck, vibrates at just one frequency to produce one particular note very accurately. Musicians match this note on their instruments with the pure sound from the fork and adjust all their other notes on the musical scale accordingly. There are several different kinds of tuning fork—each produces a different note.

THE SCIENCE OF SOUND

27

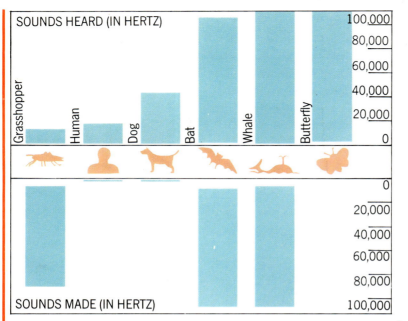

SOUNDS HEARD (IN HERTZ)

Grasshopper
Human
Dog
Bat
Whale
Butterfly

100,000
80,000
60,000
40,000
20,000
0

0
20,000
40,000
60,000
80,000
100,000

SOUNDS MADE (IN HERTZ)

Left: *Here you can see the range of sounds that are made and can be heard by different animals. Most animals can hear a much greater range of sounds than they can make. Butterflies make no sound at all and yet they can hear frequencies greater than 100,000 Hertz. Whales and bats both have very sensitive ears. Compared with these animals humans have very poor hearing. Grasshoppers are unusual insects; they can hear only a tiny proportion of the sounds that they make.*

The person in the picture below hears the echo of his voice from the closer wall before the echo from the distant wall. The farther the sound must travel, the more time it takes.
Inset: *Bats find their food by making high-pitched squeaks that we cannot hear. As the sounds hit the insect, an echo bounces back to the bat's large ears.*

Hearing sound

Humans can hear only a small proportion of the sounds in the world. Animals such as dogs and bats are much more sensitive to very high-pitched sounds than humans are. Whales and dolphins communicate with very low frequency sounds and use echoes of high sounds for navigation.

An **echo** is reflected sound waves. You can hear an echo of your voice if you shout loudly at a rock face or high wall some distance away. A short time passes between your shout and the echo because sound waves take about a second to travel 1,000 feet through air. Sound travels much faster through liquids and solids. For example, it travels four times as fast in water as in air.

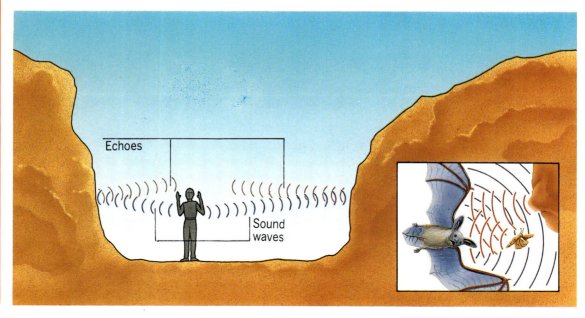

Echoes

Sound waves

Controlling sound

Sound echoes have many vital uses. Ships have "sonar" equipment that can send high-pitched sounds down through the water and measure the time it takes for the sound to be bounced back off the seabed. The readings are used to calculate the distance the sound has traveled and so work out the depth of the sea. A hospital "ultrasound" scanner uses very high-pitched—ultra—sounds, which are beyond our hearing range, to "look" inside a person's body. The reflected sounds are then displayed on a screen in the form of a picture.

Hard surfaces are the best reflectors of sounds. If you are someone who sings in the bathroom, you will know that the sounds echo—"reverberate"—around the tiled walls. But try singing in the living room, and you will find that there are no echoes because the sounds are absorbed by soft curtains, furniture, and carpets. Acoustics is a branch of science concerned with controlling sound. In an office, the acoustics must be designed to prevent telephones, typewriters, and computers from disturbing people. In very noisy workplaces, such as factories, people should wear ear protectors, because loud noise can damage the ears.

A good concert hall is one that is designed so that the only sounds which are reflected to the audience are those which help them to hear the music clearly. Some reverberation improves the sound of music, but too much can spoil it if the sounds overlap one another. Circular buildings have special properties to reflect sounds and focus them at certain points. The round amphitheaters built by ancient Greeks were designed so that every member of the audience, which numbered many thousands, could hear the voices of the actors clearly.

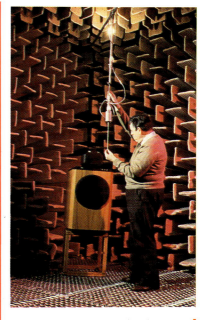

Above: *Special materials are used in concert halls and recording studios to absorb certain sounds and reflect others. The studio has rather odd-looking "acoustic tiles" on the walls.*
Below: *This nurse is using a scanner to send ultrasounds into the abdomen of a pregnant woman. The reflected sounds form a picture of the developing baby on a screen, that can be studied.*

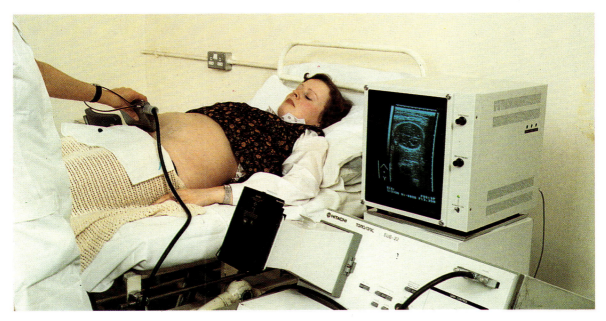

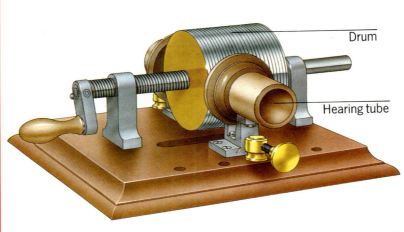

Drum

Hearing tube

Recording sound

In 1877 Thomas Edison produced a hand operated "phono-gram" that played recordings made on tinfoil cylinders. This century has seen the invention of clockwork machines that played flat discs at 78 rpm (revolutions per minute). These "78" records, made of shellac, were the first to be mass-produced from one master disc. Later came record players powered by electricity, long-playing records (33⅓ rpm), tape and cassette players, personal stereos that we can listen to through headphones and compact discs. Today recorded sound quality is almost as clear as the original sound.

In order to make a recording, sound vibrations must be converted into a form that can be stored. The whole process of recording sound onto vinyl discs begins at the microphone. This turns sound into bursts of electric

Edison's phonogram recorded sounds by making impressions of the sound vibrations on tin foil wrapped around the hand-turned brass drum. A thin "diaphragm" inside the recording tube vibrated and made a stylus mark the foil. To play back the sound, another stylus moved along the impressions as the drum turned and sound came out of the hearing tube. Edison made the first recording of a human voice—himself reciting the poem "Mary had a little lamb."

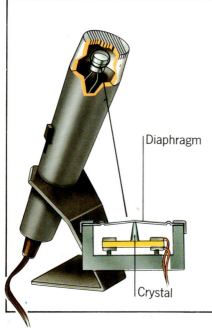

Diaphragm

Crystal

In a microphone, sound waves hit a thin plate (diaphragm) and make it vibrate. The diaphragm is attached to a device (in our example a crystal) that responds to the diaphragm's vibrations and turns them into electrical signals. A loudspeaker (right) turns signals back into sounds. A metal coil inside a magnet vibrates as signals reach it. This makes the magnet vibrate, which in turn vibrates a plastic cone. The cone produces sounds.

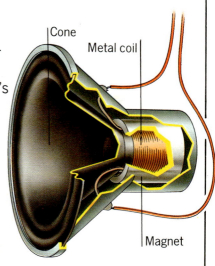

Cone

Metal coil

Magnet

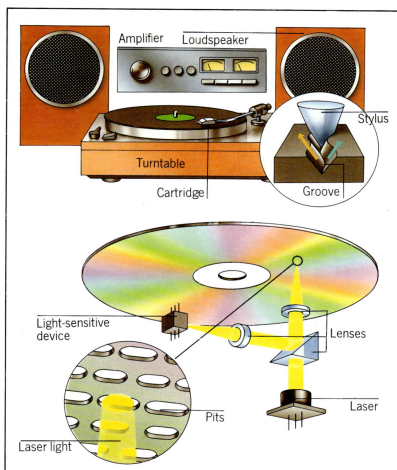

Amplifier Loudspeaker

Turntable

Cartridge

Stylus

Groove

Light-sensitive device

Lenses

Pits

Laser

Laser light

RECORDS AND DISCS

A modern record player has a turntable that spins records at a speed of 45 or 33⅓ revolutions per minute (rpm). The "arm" holds a stylus and a cartridge. The tip of the stylus is made of diamond or sapphire. It vibrates as it follows the groove of the record (inset). This causes the cartridge to produce electrical signals that pass to the amplifier and to the loudspeaker.

A compact disc player uses lenses and mirrors to reflect a laser beam off the disc's surface. This beam carries information from pits in the surface. A light-sensitive device receives this information which is turned into sounds.

current called "signals." The signals, which vary according to the loudness and frequency of the sound, are passed to an "amplifier," which makes them powerful enough to "cut" a record. A special cutting needle called a "stylus" vibrates in tune with the signals it receives and marks the pattern of signals into the sides of a groove in a soft, plastic master disc. From this one disc many more records can be "pressed" (copied). To make a cassette tape, the electrical signals are converted into bands of magnetic pattern on the surface of a tape. A compact disc stores information in millions of tiny pits on the surface of the disc.

When we listen to recordings, the record, disc or cassette players we use convert the stored messages back, firstly to electrical signals and then to vibrations of air that we can hear. A record player picks up the stored messages with a stylus and cartridge, a cassette player has sensitive magnetic heads which the tape is wound around, and compact discs are "read" by laser beams. The electric signals that these devices produce are fed to the amplifier inside the players which makes them strong enough to vibrate the loudspeaker. The loudspeaker's vibrations are passed onto the air and the vibrating air hits our ears as sound.

Older sound systems produced sound from just one loudspeaker. This "mono" sound travels to the listener from just one direction. More recent "stereo" equipment carries sound through two channels to be reproduced by two speakers. It gives an impression of sound coming from all around.

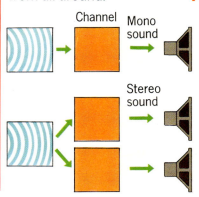

Channel

Mono sound

Stereo sound

4. Light and Color

During the daytime, our world is lit by powerful light rays from the sun which travel to us across 93 million miles of space. At night we turn on artificial electric lights. But even the most powerful electric light beam can travel no more than a few hundred yards.

The light we can see is only part of the enormous amount of energy which the sun gives out in the form of **electromagnetic waves**. As well as visible light, infrared (heat) waves, ultraviolet (UV) rays, radio waves, X-rays, and gamma waves travel to earth. (You can find out more about electromagnetic waves on page 42.) All the waves travel at a speed of 186,000 miles per second, which means that it only takes about eight minutes for them to travel from the sun to us.

Light travels much faster than sound. During a thunderstorm, lightning and thunder occur at the same time, but you see the lightning before you hear the thunder because the light waves reach you before the sound waves.

The color of light

The light we see appears to be colorless, but sunlight can be split into red, orange, yellow, green, blue, indigo, and violet. Isaac Newton was the first to do this in 1665 when

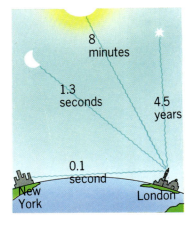

It takes 8 minutes for light to reach us from the sun. We measure distances in space in "light years." A light year is the distance light travels in one year. The nearest star is 4.5 light years away.

Lightning reaches us in a fraction of a second. Thunder takes about five seconds to travel one mile. To work out how many miles away a storm is, count the seconds between the lightning and the thunder and divide this by five.

he shone light through a specially-cut piece of glass called a "prism." He called the rainbow of colors that he saw a "spectrum." Light splits into this spectrum when it is bent. It bends as it passes from one substance to another—in this case from air to glass. Look at the sunny sky after a rainstorm. The arched rainbow of colors that sometimes forms is produced by drops of moisture in the damp air acting like prisms and splitting up the beams of sunlight.

Seeing color

We see color because the light-sensitive layer (the retina) in our eyes has special cells which respond to red, blue, and green light. These are three **primary** colors and all the colors we see are combinations of them. Colored objects don't produce light themselves, they reflect the light which shines on them back into our eyes. The color they reflect is the color that they appear. White objects reflect all the light that shines on them, green things reflect only the green part of the spectrum and absorb the rest, while black objects reflect hardly any light at all.

People can see all the colors of the rainbow (unless they are color-blind), but dogs, cats, and most other mammals cannot recognize color at all. Birds, reptiles, fish, and insects can distinguish colors and some of them are sensitive to waves which we cannot "see." For example, bees can "see" ultraviolet waves and some snakes respond to infrared rays.

In this illustration, the white light being shone through a glass prism is bending at the boundary between the air and glass. Each color in the rainbow of colors that make up white light has waves of a different length, the red waves bend the least and violet the most. Shining white light into the prism splits up the spectrum of colors. The same effect is seen in a rainbow.

MIXING LIGHT

1. Mixing different combinations of the primary light colors produces any color. All three mixed produce white.

2. But the main colors of pigments (such as paint) are different because they reflect the primary colors. They give any color except white. All three mixed produce black.

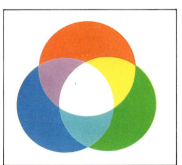

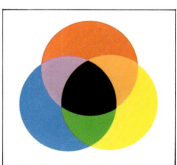

Left: Objects look a certain color because they reflect part of the spectrum and absorb the rest.

Bending light with mirrors and lenses

We all know that normally it's impossible to see around corners. Rays of light travel in straight lines and cannot bend around corners. Think about sunbeams shining through the trees or the beam of light from a torch. But if you look in a mirror you can see your face because light rays are bounced back to you—**reflected**—by the mirror. A mirror is a sheet of smooth glass coated on the back with a shiny metal (to stop light rays from passing straight through), but any flat shiny surface, such as a clear pond or polished table, can reflect light from its straight path. A special instrument called a periscope (see opposite page) uses the fact that light rays are reflected off mirrors in order to let us look around corners or over obstacles.

The image of any object in a mirror is back to front, but in a flat mirror it is not changed in size. However, mirrors that curve outward in the center—**convex** mirrors—give smaller images than those you see in a flat mirror. For example, driving mirrors in cars are convex. They reflect light from objects which are far apart and so allow drivers to see a large area of the road behind them. **Concave** mirrors curve inward at the center. They produce enlarged images of nearby objects, such as a person's face, and so are used for shaving or applying makeup. Huge, very concave mirrors are used inside astronomical telescopes to collect light from great distances so that we can

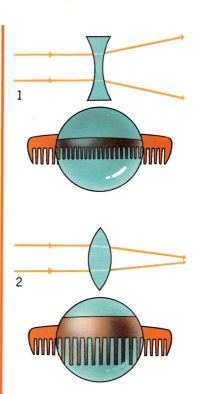

Above: 1. A "biconcave" lens has two concave faces. It makes light beams spread out and so things look smaller. 2. A lens with two convex surfaces makes beams converge and magnifies objects.

Light enters our eyes through a small hole—the pupil—in the center. If the light is very bright the pupil becomes smaller, if it is dark, the pupil opens to let in more light.

A CARDBOARD CAMERA

1. Paint the inside of a box (such as a shoe box), including the lid, black. Cut out a square from one side and stick tracing paper over the opening. Make a small hole in the opposite side of the box.
2. Aim your "viewer" at a well-lit object. An upsidedown image of the object appears on the screen. This is because light rays travel in straight lines from an object and cross as

they pass through the hole. If photographic paper is used instead of tracing paper, your viewer becomes a simple camera.

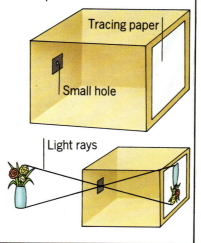

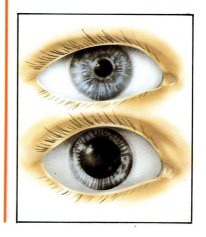

study stars millions of miles away (see page 36).

Light travels at different speeds through different transparent substances. At the boundary between two materials it changes speed slightly and is diverted—**refracted**—from its straight path. You will see the strange effect of refraction if you hold a pencil so that part of it is behind a thick glass. Light travels more slowly through glass than it does through air. So light rays coming from the pencil change direction at the glass, and the pencil appears to separate into two parts.

Lenses are special pieces of glass, with at least one curved surface, that bend light rays passing through them by refraction. Magnifying glasses are convex lenses which bulge out in the center. They make light rays "converge" —come closer together—to a point called a "focus." There is a convex lens in each of our eyes which focuses light on the light-sensitive retina at the back of our eyeballs. Concave lenses are thin at the center and thick at the edges. Looking through them makes things look smaller because they make rays of light "diverge"— spread out.

Lenses bend each of the colors of the spectrum by a slightly different amount, just as a prism does. Usually the effect is too small to see, but in optical instruments such as telescopes and binoculars, a fringe of unwanted colors can interefere with the view. This coloration, called "chromatic aberration," can be overcome by using two lenses of different shapes and types of glass, fixed together. The second lens recombines any colors produced by the first. These combination lenses are said to be "achromatic"

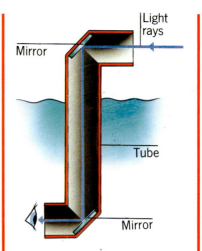

Above: *A submarine periscope like the one in the photograph allows people below water to see an object above it. Light from the object is reflected off the top mirror, down the tube onto another mirror and into the eye.*

Right: *1. Place a coin in a dish. Move back until you cannot see it. Now ask someone to pour some water into the dish. Light rays from the coin are bent (refracted) toward your eyes as they pass through water—bringing the coin into view.*

2. Here, the paintbrush seems to bend because light from it is refracted as it passes from the air into water. The brush also looks slightly bigger because the glass gives the water a curved shape, so that it acts as a magnifying lens.

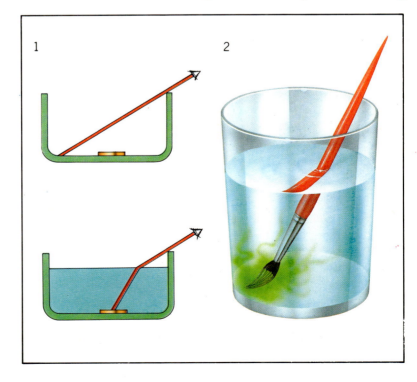

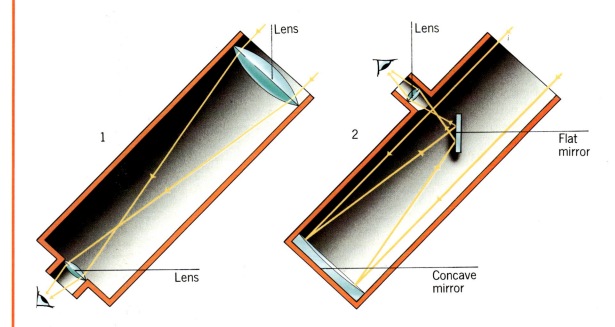

1

2

Lens

Lens

Lens

Flat mirror

Concave mirror

Telescopes and microscopes

Before the invention of the telescope, astronomers could only observe the sun and stars with the naked eye. Hans Lippershey, a Dutch spectacle maker, built the first telescope in 1608. This revealed details of planets and moons never dreamed of before. But it was the Italian astronomer Galileo Galilei who gave the telescope its name, which means "to see things at a distance." His **refracting** (lens) telescope, made in 1610, was able to magnify 30 times. Refracting telescopes have a large front lens called the "objective." This lens collects far more light than our eyes can, and makes an enlarged image inside the tube of the telescope. A second smaller lens—the "eyepiece" —magnifies this image.

Early refracting telescopes suffered from chromatic aberration (see page 35) which gave images a rainbow-colored edge. In 1668 Isaac Newton solved this problem by building a **reflecting** telescope, which used a concave mirror instead of an objective lens. The enlarged image produced by the concave mirror is reflected in a second, flat mirror and then through an eyepiece lens into the viewer's eye. However, achromatic lenses which do not give colored edges to their images were invented in the mid 1700s, so both reflecting and refracting telescopes are still used today. About 40 years ago, radio telescopes were invented. These telescopes gather the radio waves (rather than light) which travel to earth from the stars.

1. A refracting telescope uses two lenses to focus rays of light from distant stars and planets.
2. Reflecting telescopes use a large concave mirror to reflect light onto a smaller mirror that passes it through a lens to the eye.

Below: *The William Herschel telescope, nearly 8000 feet above the Atlantic on La Palma, the Canaries, is the world's most powerful reflecting telescope. Its mirror is nearly 14 feet across.*

Microscopes

Telescopes let us study enormous planets and stars which we cannot see because they are too far away. Microscopes reveal objects which are very close to us, but so small that they are invisible to the naked eye. Microscopes were first used in the 1600s to look at small insects and cells. Today, scientists use "light" microscopes that can enlarge objects several thousand times, so that even the smallest bacteria can be seen. Electron microscopes are even more powerful. They enlarge objects up to a million times by using a beam of electrons (charged atomic particles) instead of light. Scientists use them to study minute objects, such as crystals of metals and viruses, that are only a fraction of a millimeter long.

The most important parts of any light microscopes are the two convex lenses used to magnify the object. The first lens—the objective—is mounted just above the "specimen" (the object being studied). The objective lens produces an enlarged image of the specimen inside the cylinder of the microscope. This image is enlarged again by the second lens—the eyepiece. In the best microscopes there may be a system of two or three eyepiece lenses to give greater magnification.

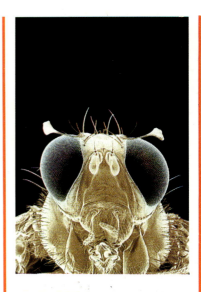

The photograph above shows the head of a fruit fly seen through a special type of electron microscope that scans the specimen to reveal three-dimensional details. The compound eyes of the fly have many individual lenses that have been tinted blue.

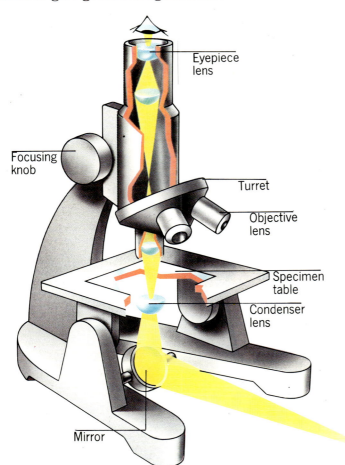

Eyepiece lens

Focusing knob

Turret

Objective lens

Specimen table

Condenser lens

Mirror

Left: *A light microscope. Light shining on a large mirror at the base is reflected upward through a condenser lens. This lens focuses light so that it passes through the specimen (the object being studied). The light rays then pass up through the objective and eyepiece lenses and into the viewer's eye. Turning the knob at the side of the microscope moves these lenses up and down to bring the specimen into focus. The turret can be turned to select one of the three lenses— each one magnifies to a different degree.*

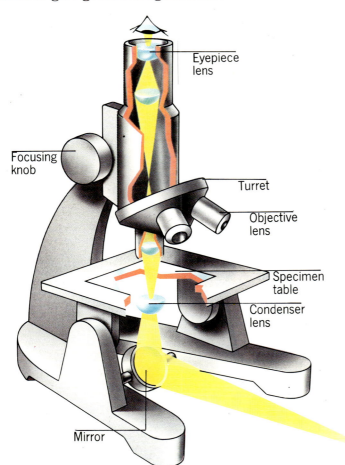

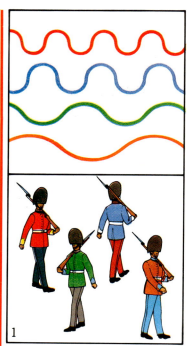

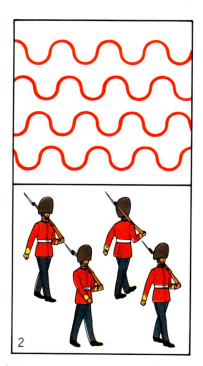

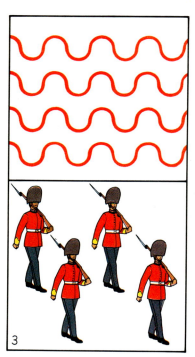

Above: *1. Ordinary white light. This light is a mixture of colors, each of which has a different wavelength. The waves are not in step (in phase) with one another. You can imagine white light as soldiers of several different regiments marching out of step. Each regiment represents a different wavelength of light.*

2. One-colored ("monochromatic") light. This light is all the same wavelength, but the waves are not in phase. This is rather like soldiers of the same regiment who are marching out of step.

3. Laser light is all the same wavelength and the waves are in phase. You can picture this as soldiers of the same regiment marching in step. Laser light is said to be "coherent" light. This is why it is so powerful and intense.

Lasers

A laser produces light, but it is very different from the light of the sun or a lamp. Sunlight is composed of light of many colors, each with a different wavelength (see page 42). Ordinary light spreads out in all directions and its beams fade as they travel. A laser beam looks like a straight rod because it is made of very intense beams which stay almost parallel and keep their intensity over very long distances. The concentrated, straight beam of laser light can be extremely powerful.

The first laser was built in 1960 from a rod of ruby. It produced red light. Today, many other materials, including the gases carbon dioxide and argon and a combination of helium and neon, are used to produce laser light of different colors and varying strength. The gas, or other material which will produce the light, is enclosed in a tube and an electric current is passed through it. This excites the atoms or molecules of the gas so that they give off tiny packets or "photons" of light energy. Some photons hit other atoms which give off more photons. The effect is increased as more and more photons are produced.

Using lasers

Just like ordinary light, laser light can be reflected and focused by mirrors and lenses. By choosing a beam of the correct power, lasers can be directed to weld or drill metal. Their intense beams produce clean round holes by vaporizing the metal. Less powerful laser beams are used in medical surgery, for example to re-attach retinas which have come away from the eyeball, or to remove warts.

Engineers use laser beams to measure distances very accurately because the rays spread out very little. All light travels at the same speed—186,000 miles per second —so by measuring the time it takes for a laser to travel between two points, the distance the beam has traveled can be calculated precisely. The parallel beams of a laser can also be used to make sure that tunnels and buildings are straight or level. Lasers have numerous other uses. These include playing compact discs (see page 31), transmitting phone calls down glass fibers (see page 40) and "reading" bar codes on products in stores. Look at the small pattern of black and white stripes on certain items in stores. This is a "bar code." If a special pen, which gives out a weak beam of laser light, is passed over this, the light is absorbed by the black areas and reflected by the white ones. This pattern of reflection is decoded into a series of product numbers which goes into a computer.

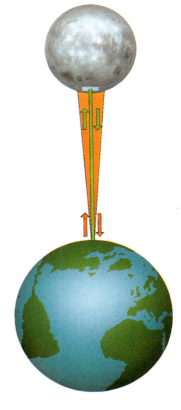

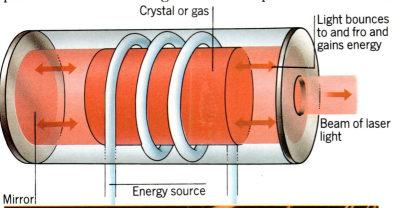

Crystal or gas

Light bounces to and fro and gains energy

Beam of laser light

Mirror

Energy source

Above: *A laser's straight beam can be reflected back to earth by a mirror on the moon. The time it takes for the beam to travel to and from the moon can be used to calculate the moon's distance from the earth to within 6 inches. A radar beam could be used, but it spreads out as it travels, and so is not as accurate.*
Above left: *A laser consists of a crystal or a tube of gas. A burst of energy is absorbed by the laser, builds up and is released as a beam of laser light.*

Left: *Laser light being used to cut through steel.*

Communicating with lasers

Since the discovery of the laser in 1960, a whole new way of sending messages and storing information has been opened up. Laser beams can be used to transmit telephone calls, television broadcasts, and computer data. They also read visual or audio information stored on special discs and are used in laser printers to make books and newspapers (see page 115).

Laser beams are powerful, but they are stopped by obstacles in their paths. In the atmosphere surrounding the earth, clouds and weather conditions obstruct them, so they cannot be used to send messages directly between two places. But in space, where there is no "weather," they carry messages between satellites. To overcome the problem back down on earth, laser beams carrying information are sent along special cables made of hair-thin glass fibers. The transmission of light down glass fibers is known as "fiber optics." Laser light can travel along one of these fibers very efficiently because the outer surface of the fibre reflects light back into the center. This means that any rays that reach the surface are deflected back inside instead of being lost.

Messages are carried along the fibers as tiny pulses of laser light. At one end of the cable, telephone, television, or computer information is turned into electrical pulses, which in turn work a laser transmitter that produces a laser beam. The beam varies in exactly the same way as the messages and pulses did. If the signals are to be sent a long distance, they have to be amplified or "boosted" along the way. Telephone cables have "repeaters"—lasers which do this about every 30 miles. At the other end of the cable, a receiver turns the light pulses back into electrical signals which can be converted to sounds or pictures once again.

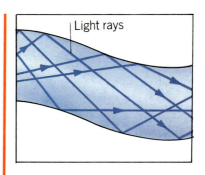

Light rays

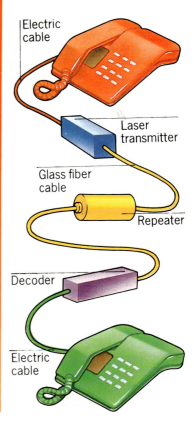

Electric cable

Laser transmitter

Glass fiber cable

Repeater

Decoder

Electric cable

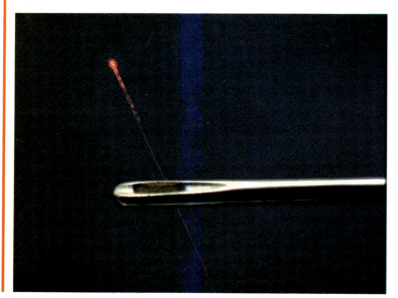

Above: *Light sent down a glass fiber is reflected back inside if it hits the surface. A bunch of 100 fibers forms a cable less than half an inch thick that can carry nearly one million telephone conversations at the same time. A transmitter turns telephone signals into pulses of laser light. Glass is cheaper and lighter than copper wire.*

Left: *A fiber passes through the eye of a needle.*

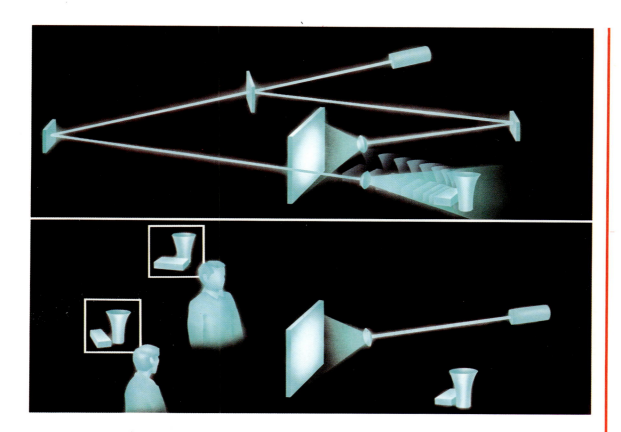

Making pictures with lasers

Holography is a way of using lasers to store information about three-dimensional objects on a flat plate. Like ordinary photography, an image is recorded and reproduced. But, unlike photography, the reproduced image is actually a "3-D" reconstruction. Holograms look so realistic because when the plate is lit by a laser, it reflects light in exactly the same way as the original object did. The pattern of light which reaches your eyes is exactly the same as that from the real object.

To make a hologram, lenses and mirrors focus laser beams to form images on a plate which is covered with a light-sensitive substance. Very basically, if laser light is shone onto an object, the object will reflect some of the rays. The light-sensitive substance records this pattern of reflected light on the plate. If a laser beam is then shone onto the plate, the image is reconstructed (see illustration above).

Holograms can only be made at the same size as the objects they record. This means they are used mainly to store information about small items. However, they are already being used, not only in advertising and entertainment, but also to keep dental records, images of works of art, and to check materials for points of weakness and stress. So far, holograms cannot give true color reproduction because their color depends on the color of the laser which was used to record and reconstruct the image.

Above top: *To make a hologram, light from a laser is divided into two beams, the "reference" and the "object" beams. The reference beam is shone directly onto the hologram plate while the object beam is reflected off the object before reaching the plate. The plate stores the patterns made by the two beams and is processed just like photographic film. Everything must be kept perfectly still—even sound can blur the image.*

Above bottom: *To view the hologram, the plate must be lit by another laser. As the beam is shone onto it, a three-dimensional image is made. Looking at the hologram from different angles gives different views —like moving around any three-dimensional object.*

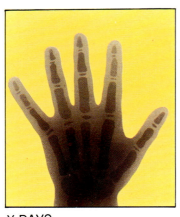

X-RAYS

RADAR

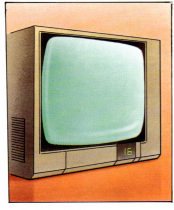

TELEVISION

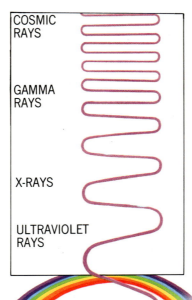

COSMIC RAYS

GAMMA RAYS

X-RAYS

ULTRAVIOLET RAYS

VISIBLE LIGHT

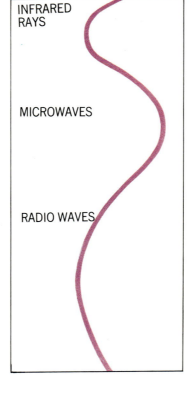

INFRARED RAYS

MICROWAVES

RADIO WAVES

ULTRAVIOLET RAYS

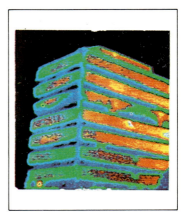

INFRARED RAYS

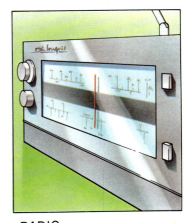

RADIO

Light beyond sight

Our universe is full of the waves of energy that make up the **electromagnetic spectrum**. These various types of wave are very important to us and yet our senses can detect only a small proportion of them. We can see ordinary visible light and feel the heat of infrared waves, but radio waves, ultraviolet (UV), and X-rays pass right

Different wavelengths of the electromagnetic spectrum are used for different things. The infrared photo shows the heat given out by an office block. White areas are hottest, red areas are warm, green cool, and blue cold.

through our bodies without us knowing it. All the waves travel at the same speed—the speed of light—but their **wavelengths** vary. Cosmic rays are less than one hundred million-millionth of a meter in length, while radio waves can be several miles long.

The radio waves that we know best are those that bring us music and speech via our radios. But there are other radio waves flashing continuously through space. Some come from distant stars, others are created by lightning. The shortest type of radio waves are microwaves. These useful beams are between 30 centimeters and less than 1 millimeter long. Microwaves pass messages between satellites and are used by radar systems (see page 45) to detect distant objects. Their most familiar use is for cooking food in microwave ovens.

The shorter waves of the electromagnetic spectrum are more penetrating and some are harmful to our bodies. Just shorter than the light we can see are the waves of ultraviolet light, produced in large amounts by the sun. Much of this UV light is absorbed by the atmosphere. It is the UV light that reaches us that gives us a tan. Our skin makes brown pigment to stop the rays from penetrating it.

Getting shorter

Next in the spectrum, with still shorter wavelengths than UV light, come X-rays. These rays can pass through human tissue but are partly stopped by dense materials such as bones and teeth. When X-rays are passed through us onto a photographic plate, bones, teeth, and some other parts show up on the plate as shadows which doctors can examine. Too much exposure to X-rays can harm body cells—some X-rays are used to kill cancer cells inside the body. People who operate X-ray machines must wear protective clothing or stand behind lead screens which absorb the rays.

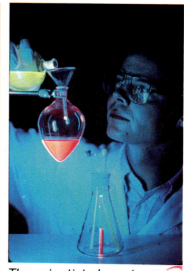

The scientist above is working with red and yellow phosphorescent substances. These glow luminously when certain electromagnetic rays are shone onto them. They go on glowing after the radiation has gone.

Below: Microwaves produced in the magnetron of a microwave oven are reflected off the oven's metal walls onto the food. These waves agitate water molecules in the food. The molecules rub against each other and the friction produces heat, which cooks the food.

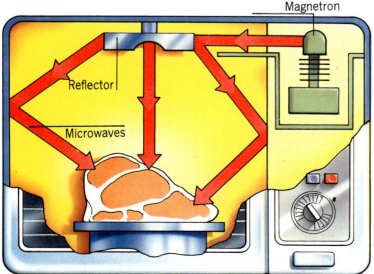

Magnetron

Reflector

Microwaves

5. Electronics

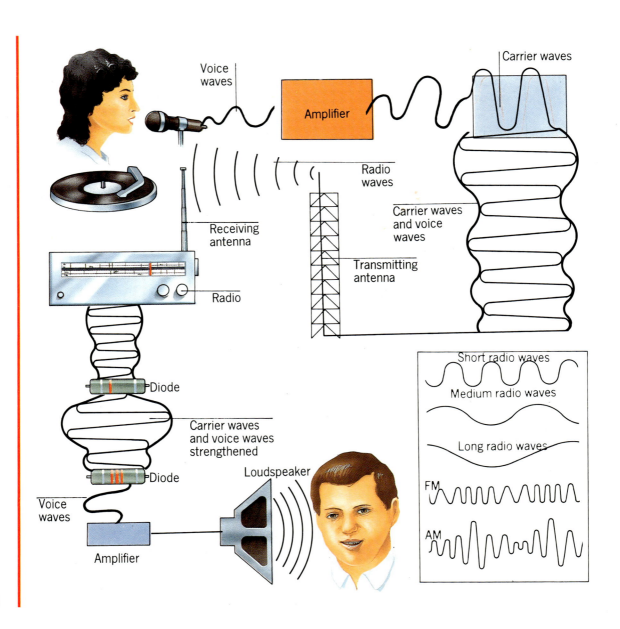

Voice waves

Amplifier

Carrier waves

Radio waves

Carrier waves and voice waves

Receiving antenna

Transmitting antenna

Radio

Diode

Carrier waves and voice waves strengthened

Diode

Loudspeaker

Voice waves

Amplifier

Short radio waves

Medium radio waves

Long radio waves

FM

AM

Radio and television

The electronic parts of a radio turn the signals sent from a radio station into sounds that we can hear. These signals are special radio waves from the electromagnetic spectrum that can be "coded" to carry sounds. The coded radio waves travel out in all directions from a transmitter and the antenna in your radio at home can collect them when the radio is switched on.

The sounds of a radio program begin their journey to your radio at the microphone. Microphones convert the sound waves (see page 27) that pass into them into electrical signals. The signals are amplified (strengthened) and sent to a transmitter. Transmitters produce special radio waves called "carrier" waves. These carrier waves have the radio signals joined to them—the radio signals "modulate" the carrier waves. Transmitter antennas radiate the carrier waves, with their signals, so that they can be picked up by a receiving antenna in a radio. Tuning your radio picks out the signal coming from the station you want to listen to from the others. Each station broadcasts on its own frequency (wavelength) so that all the stations don't get muddled up together. Inside a radio, signals are separated from their carrier waves and then turned back into sounds by the loudspeaker.

The station selector on your radio may have the initials AM and FM on it. These initials tell you how the carrier wave was joined with the signals at the transmitter. AM stands for "amplitude modulation." This means that the amplitude (height) of the carrier waves was altered to match the signals. FM—"frequency modulation"—means that the frequency—the number of carrier waves passing each second—was changed to match the signal at the transmitter.

Broadcasting stations use "long," "medium" and "short" waves. Long and medium waves are between 10,000 and 100 meters long. (The wavelength of waves becomes shorter as their frequency becomes higher.) These waves tend to follow the curve of the earth's surface and are useful for distances up to about 700 miles. But short waves between 10 and 100 meters long bounce off a layer called the "ionosphere" high up in the atmosphere (see page 21). The waves are reflected back down to earth, far from the transmitter. Because of this, short waves are used for long-distance broadcasting. VHF ("very high frequency" waves) and UHF ("ultra high frequency" waves) travel straight through the ionosphere into outer space. Astronauts and space satellites use them. VHF transmitters with a very short range on earth often use frequency modulation.

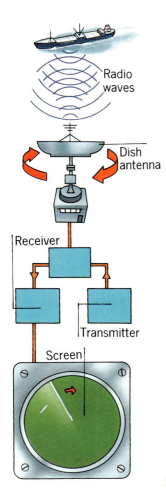

Above: *Radar (**ra**dio **de**tection **an**d **r**anging) locates objects by using very short radio waves. The rotating dish antenna sends out signals from the transmitter that bounce back off objects in their path. The returning signals are decoded by a receiver that shows the direction and distance of the objects as "blips" on a screen. Large objects reflect waves the best so radar is most often used to locate ships and for air traffic control.*

Left: *How a radio broadcast is carried to your radio.*

Television

A television programme begins wherever a camera films an event. Color television cameras use special mirrors to divide the light they receive into three primary colours —red, blue, and green. Combinations of these colors can produce any other colors in our televisions. Beams of the three colors are turned into electronic signals. These are transmitted on very high frequency carrier waves in a similar way to radio broadcasts (see page 44). Television waves are very short radio waves and are not reflected back to earth by the atmosphere—they just shoot off into space. So, if "live" television pictures need to be sent a long way, for example from New York to London, the waves are sent up to a satellite high above the earth (see page 21). This satellite reflects them back down to a special dish antenna in London.

The television in your home has an antenna which picks up carrier waves and their signals. You can select the

Below: How television works. Signals from the television camera are sent out by a transmitting antenna and picked up by your antenna. The inside of your television screen is coated with chemical phosphor dots. Farther back is a "gun" that fires electrons onto the back of the screen when it receives a signal. This makes the dots glow and combinations of these dots form a picture. A color television has three guns—one for each of light's primary colors.

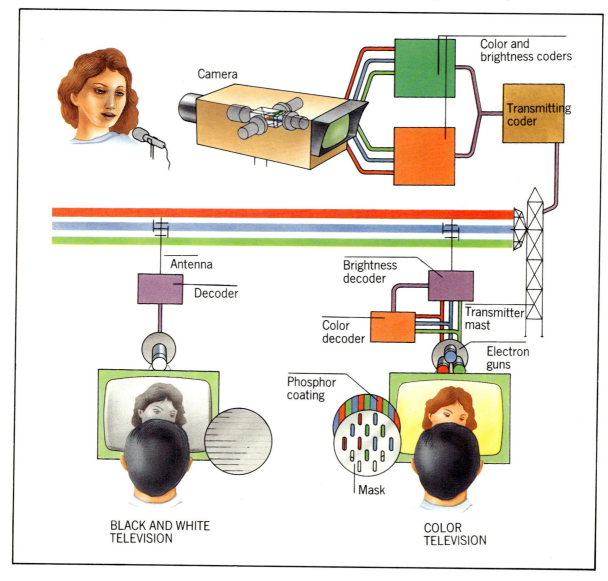

Camera

Color and brightness coders

Transmitting coder

Antenna

Decoder

Brightness decoder

Color decoder

Transmitter mast

Electron guns

Phosphor coating

Mask

BLACK AND WHITE TELEVISION

COLOR TELEVISION

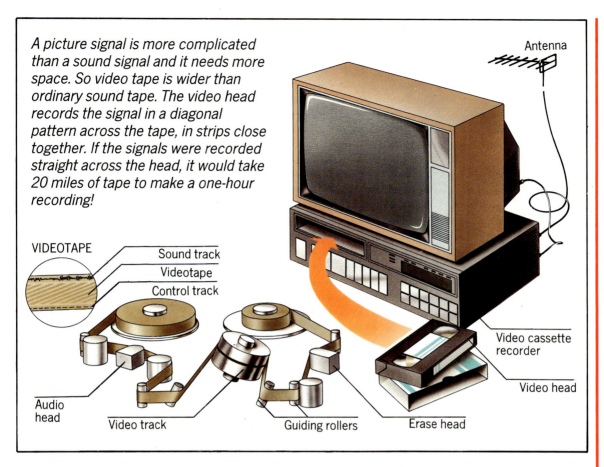

A picture signal is more complicated than a sound signal and it needs more space. So video tape is wider than ordinary sound tape. The video head records the signal in a diagonal pattern across the tape, in strips close together. If the signals were recorded straight across the head, it would take 20 miles of tape to make a one-hour recording!

Antenna

VIDEOTAPE

Sound track
Videotape
Control track

Audio head

Video track

Guiding rollers

Erase head

Video cassette recorder

Video head

station you want to watch by tuning the television to allow through waves that are of the frequency of that station. The signals are turned back into sound by the speaker, and into pictures by the "tube." The only part of the tube that you can see is the television screen. At the back, away from the screen, the tube has three electron guns. Each gun fires a stream of electrons in response to one of the three color signals from the original camera. The screen is coated on the inside with a pattern of phosphor* dots that glow as electrons hit them. A green signal makes a green spot on the screen, a blue signal gives a blue spot and so on. As combinations of the colored dots glow on the screen a TV picture is formed.

*See page 43

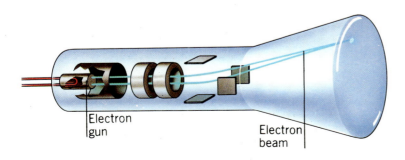

Electron gun

Electron beam

Above: *A video cassette recorder receives signals through a cable connected to the television antenna. Rollers guide the videotape past "heads" in the recorder. To record, an erase head removes any existing material and a video head records new picture signals as a diagonal pattern on the magnetic tape. Sound signals are recorded along one edge of the tape by the audio head.*
Left: *Your television screen is actually the wide end of a cathode ray tube. The electron guns are at the narrow end. The tube is made of glass and has the air pumped out of it because electron beams can pass easily through a vacuum.*

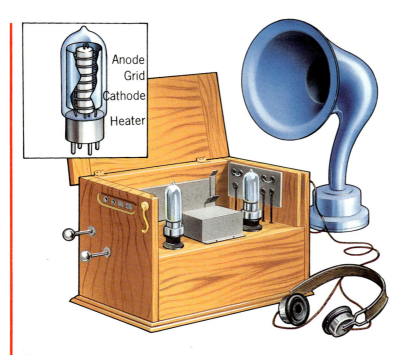

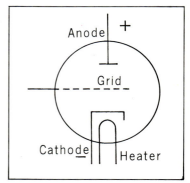

Left: *Old-fashioned radios had to be large to hold big glass tubes.*

Below: *The symbol used in diagrams of electrical circuits to represent a triode tube.*

Tubes and transistors

Before we can enjoy the sounds and pictures from signals gathered by our radio and television antennas, the signals need to be amplified. The signals must make changes in the flow of electricity strong enough to make the radio or television speaker vibrate. Early radios and televisions had large glass **tubes** to control the flow of electricity and amplify signals.

One type of tube used as an amplifier was called a "triode." As its name tells us, it had three main parts—a **cathode**, an **anode**, and a wire mesh between them called a grid. As electric current flows to heat up the cathode, negatively charged electrons stream from it through the grid to the anode. Signals from the antenna go to the grid and make it either more positively or more negatively charged. A negative charge repels the stream of electrons from the cathode and prevents electric current from flowing. A positive charge attracts electrons and allows a strong current to flow. Even tiny changes in the charge on the grid cause big changes in electric current

Below: *Sections through two transistors. The arrows represent the flow of electricity. If a transistor is made of two pieces of silicon, electricity can flow in one direction but not back again. Transistors like this act like diode tubes ("di" means "two") and change AC into DC (see page 66/7). The other transistor is made of a sandwich of three differently treated pieces of silicon. The center of the sandwich works like the grid of a triode tube, so the transistor amplifies the signal.*

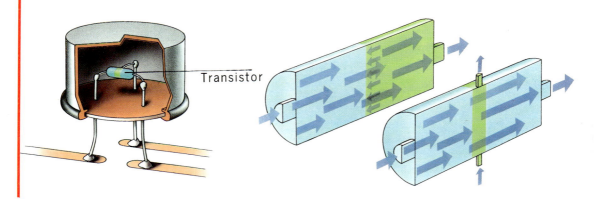

Transistor

and so the signal is amplified. Because these tubes are large, the radios and televisions had to be large and clumsy too.

Smaller radios and televisions were made possible by the invention of the **transistor** in 1947. Transistors do just what tubes do, but they are smaller, cheaper, and more reliable. Transistors consist of a sandwich of three specially treated pieces of silicon. Silicon is a "semi-conducting" material, which means that it allows electricity to flow through it, but not as easily as a **conductor** such as copper does.

Discovering the silicon chip

The first "transistor" radios in the 1950s contained transistors as separate parts joined together by wires to form an electrical circuit. But by 1960, it had been discovered that different components, including microscopic transistors, could be put together into just one little piece—or **chip**—of silicon to form a whole electrical circuit. These complete—"integrated"—circuits opened the way for tiny radios, pocket calculators, and "micro" computers.

The silicon that is used to make chips is produced from a special type of sand. It is melted at 2,000°F and long cylindrical crystals, 4 inches in diameter and a yard long, are grown from it. These cylinders are sliced into thin wafers, each of which is divided into 500 chips, a quarter of an inch square. Each of these chips has tiny transistors and connecting channels "etched" onto it, using metals and other materials which stick to the surface of the chip. The process is repeated many times to give several layers of parts and produce a complete circuit.

Above: *One silicon chip compared to the size of a cherry. Silicon is a semi-conductor—it does not conduct electricity well. So tiny patches of certain other materials are built into the chip's surface. These patches are the equivalent of all the parts of an electrical circuit, including transistors.*

Below: *Just one stage in the long process of etching electronic circuits onto the chips.*

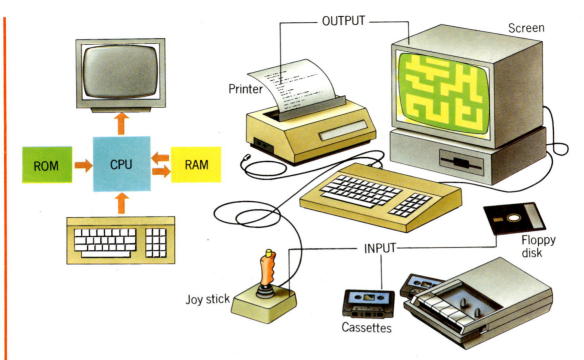

OUTPUT

Screen

Printer

ROM → CPU ⇄ RAM

Joy stick

INPUT

Floppy disk

Cassettes

The computer "revolution"

Without the silicon chip, the "computer age" would never have come about. Early computers needed thousands of separate transistors wired together. Even simple computers had to be enormous—they filled whole rooms—to hold all the required parts. Computers aren't "cleverer" than people—just faster. They can do millions of calculations each second.

All computers work in more or less the same way. They have four basic parts—the "input," the "memory," the "central processing unit" (CPU), and the "output." The input is usually a keyboard, like that on a typewriter. It is used to feed a **program** of instructions into the computer, and also data (information) such as numbers or words. The data and instructions go to a part of the computer's memory called the **RAM**. Here they are stored until they are ready to be used by the central processing unit. There is another part of the computer's memory called the **ROM**. This memory unit contains instructions that operate the central processing unit.

The CPU takes the instructions and data from the memory and carries out a calculation. The result is sent back to the memory to wait until it is needed. When required, the CPU orders the result to be sent to the output unit—a screen or a printer.

Inside the computer, every instruction and every piece of data given to it, whether this is numbers or words, is

Above: *Computers store data and programs on RAM and ROM chips. The cheapest method is to store data on a cassette that can be connected to the computer when it is needed. However, this can be slow—it may take several minutes to read a program and find data. Floppy disks are faster. They store information on magnetic disks in concentric tracks. Each track is divided into sectors so that data can be located quickly. A C60 (one hour) cassette could store all the words in this book but a 5-inch diameter floppy disk could store up to three times this amount.*

Above: *Some of the many everyday things that use chips. Watches and calculators, cash registers, bank cash dispensers, and car dashboard displays are examples.*

changed into **binary** code—a number system that has only two numerals, 0 and 1 (see box below). The computer does all its work in binary code. When the final result is produced, the computer changes it into a form we can understand, such as words or numbers.

Talking to the computer

To perform any task, a computer has to follow a set of instructions called a program. The instructions required by the central processing unit must be in binary code. Binary code is difficult to write into a program, so computer programmers use special computer languages instead. These languages use ordinary words and numbers, and the computer can turn these into its own binary code. The language used for most home computers is called BASIC.

The program below shows how even the simplest task, such as adding two numbers together, must be broken down into a series of instructions for the computer. Each line must have a number.

```
10   INPUT A
20   INPUT B
30   LET C=A+B
40   PRINT C
```

Line 10 tells the computer that you are going to "enter" (type in) a number, for example 4. The computer stores this in its memory. Then it goes to line 20 to wait for another number. Suppose you type 5. As soon as 5 is entered, the computer goes to the next line, 30. It takes the two numbers from its memory, adds them and sends the result back to memory. Then it goes to line 40, which tells it to take the result from memory and send it to the screen. The result is shown—9. Programs for more complicated tasks contain many more instructions and may be hundreds of lines long.

0	∅	∅	∅	∅
1	∅	∅	∅	1
2	∅	∅	1	∅
3	∅	∅	1	1
4	∅	1	∅	∅
5	∅	1	∅	1
6	∅	1	1	∅
7	∅	1	1	1
8	1	∅	∅	∅

Computers can only work on information in the form of binary code. This number system uses only 1s and 0s, indicated by electrical pulses. A 0 = no pulse and 1 = a pulse. From right to left, the first column stands for units of 1, the second for 2s and so on.

ELECTRONICS

The robots in the photograph on the right are assembling cars in a factory. Each robot is programmed to complete a specific task in the process as cars pass along the production line.

Shoulder swivel

Elbow extension

Arm sweep

Pitch

Roll

Yaw

Robots—computers on the move

Ask most people what a robot is and they will describe a metal model of a human that moves in a jerky way and speaks in an automatic, computerized voice. In reality, modern robots are nothing like this. They are simply electronically controlled machines that can be programmed to work for us. They do not look like metal people, nor do they speak. A robot's work may be very precise or it may require great strength. Some perform tasks that are dangerous for people, such as handling radioactive material or investigating unexploded bombs. Others do repetitive boring work such as packing, welding, or paint spraying on factory production lines.

The word "robot" comes from a Slavic word "rabota," which means work. People began using robot to mean an automated machine after a Czech writer called Karel Capek wrote a play called *Rossum's Universal Robots* in 1920. Rossum was a man whose factory built people-like machines to do the work of humans.

Today's robots do not look anything like Rossum's. Most of them have just one "arm" which has joints similar to our shoulder, wrist, and elbow joints. This arrangement gives them the ability to move in six different ways, and with the correct instructions, a robot arm can make

Above: *A typical robot. The joints in the robot's "arm" allow it to swivel at the "shoulder," to extend its "elbow" and to move its "wrist" in three directions. The gripper that forms the hand can be used for lifting objects.*

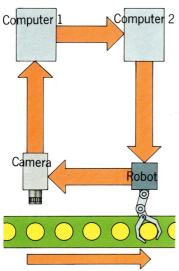

Above: How "second generation" robots respond to changing circumstances. A camera feeds information about objects on the production line to computer 1 which processes the information and passes it to computer 2. If an object is missing or faulty, computer 2 can give the robot new instructions.

movements that are extremely accurate. Some robot arms are moved by electric motors at each joint, others have compressed air systems or use compressed liquid (hydraulics) to move them. The "hand" at the end of the arm is designed to suit the job to be done. For example, a magnetic hand can pick up metal, a scoop can sample soil, and claws can hold different tools, so the robot may paint on one day and tighten screws on another.

Before a robot can do any work it has to be taught exactly what to do. All robots are controlled by computers. The instructions written by the computer programmer must first tell the robot where it is and where the parts it must pick up or move are, then it must tell the robot precisely how to move. Some robots are "taught" by moving their arm through a sequence of work in slow motion so that each step can be entered into the computer's memory. The way the arm moves depends on the job to be done. For welding or lifting, the robot may move from one spot to the next in a series of jerks. But for painting and spraying, the movements have to be smooth and continuous to give a perfect finish.

More sophisticated "second generation" robots have simple sensors so that they can gather extra information about what is happening around them and react to it. The most common sensors are cameras which give the robot "vision" so that it can stop working if a production line breaks down or when a job is completed.

ROBOTS ON FILM

The robots we see in films are the imaginative inventions of writers, producers, and modelmakers. Many of the robots are made to look like humans and they are often portrayed as sinister or threatening to ordinary people.

Above: a female robot from the film *Metropolis*, and a Dalek.
Left: Two friendly robots—CP30 and R2D2 from the 1980 film, *The Empire Strikes Back.*

6. On the Move

Objects cannot start or stop moving by themselves, they need a force to push or pull them. One such force is **gravity**, a natural force that pulls everything toward the earth. In order to produce the forces needed to move things, people have invented various machines to help them. Some machines, such as cars, lifts, and cranes, have complicated parts and need electricity or gasoline to drive them. Others are very simple and rely only on muscle power. Levers, pulleys, slopes, and wheels are all examples of simple labor-saving "machines." They are called machines because they let us get more movement for less personal effort.

Levers

Levers are among the oldest machines. They were used as long ago as 300 B.C. The simplest kind of lever is a rigid bar that rests over a pivot (a balancing point) somewhere along its length. A crowbar is a simple lever. One end of the lever must be placed under the load to be moved, and a

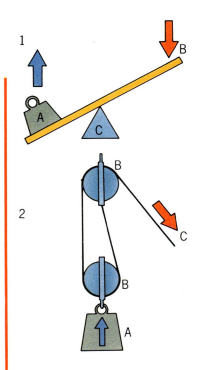

1. The lever being used to lift the load (A) is balanced at the pivot (C). The lifting force is applied at B.
2. A double "block and tackle," a device that uses two pulleys, each mounted in a frame called a block. The more pulleys (B) that are used, the less distance the load (A) travels for the same length of pull on (C). This means that less effort is needed to lift (A).
Left: Mobile cranes like this use several pulleys.

pushing force is needed at the other end. The closer the pivot is to the load, the smaller the lifting force that is required to lift it. A wheelbarrow also works on the lever principle. It is called a "second class" lever because it has its load between the balancing point—the wheel—and the handles where the lifting force is needed.

Pulleys and ramps

Two other simple machines which you can see being used almost every day are pulleys and ramps (slopes). Ramps are used to help move things from one level to another. It is much easier to drag or push something up a slope than it is to lift it up a series of steps.

Pulleys—used on building projects around 2,500 years ago—are often used on modern building sites to lift bricks and buckets. A pulley is a grooved wheel which turns on an axle. A rope passed through the groove has the load on one end and a person pulling on the other end. Double pulleys, which have two wheels, reduce the amount of effort the person must use, although he or she must pull the rope down a greater distance than the load travels up. It is easier to exert a smaller force over a great distance than a larger force over a short distance.

Isaac Newton (1642–1727) "discovered" gravity, supposedly when a falling apple hit him on the head. The greater the force used to fire this cannon ball, the farther the ball can travel before being pulled to earth by gravity. With massive force, the ball travels even farther, but gravity stops it shooting off into space.

Above: *Ramps were used as long ago as 2500 B.C. when the pyramids of Egypt were built. Slaves dragged huge stone slabs up smooth slopes to heights as great as 460 feet.*

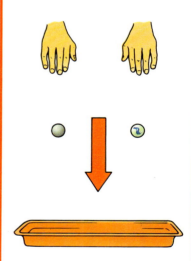

In the 1500s, Galileo, the famous Italian scientist, found that falling objects gather speed. He proposed that objects of the same size and shape fall at the same speed no matter what they weigh. Try this: drop two objects of the same size but different weights onto a tray at the same moment. Listen to see which one lands first.

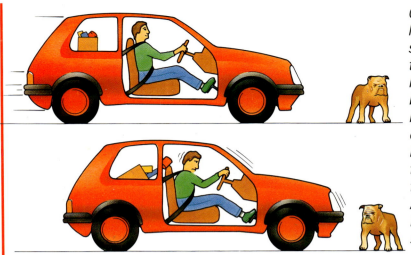

On the left you can see what happens when a car has to stop suddenly. The inertia of the driver's body has thrown him forward. Wearing seat belts makes traveling safer because they hold the driver and passengers back in their seats and prevent them from being thrown toward the windshield. Anything that is not held back, like the bag of shopping, is not so lucky.

Holding back

Why is it harder work to try and push a stationary car than it is to keep it moving once it has started to roll? The answer lies in the car's **inertia**. Inertia means "lazy" —things do not want to start moving if they are still, nor do they want to stop if they have started to move. To start something moving, or to stop it moving, we must overcome its inertia. The heavier an object is, the greater its inertia. Watch the effects of inertia on the passengers in a bus. If the bus starts moving suddenly, people tend to fall backward, because their bodies want to stay still. When the bus stops quickly, people are thrown forward as their inertia tries to keep them moving.

Friction is another force that tries to stop movement. It is produced when two surfaces rub against one another. The rougher the two surfaces, the greater the friction which is produced and the more movement is prevented. Try rubbing two sheets of sandpaper together, then rub two sheets of smooth card over one another and notice the difference. There is a lot more friction between the rough sheets of sandpaper, making them hard to move over each other. Friction can be a very useful force. In winter, grit spread on icy roads stops us slipping and cars from skidding. Tires, running shoes, and boots all have "tread" on them for the same reason—by increasing friction we stop unwanted movement between surfaces and get a better grip.

In other situations it is important to reduce the amount of friction between two surfaces because friction has two damaging side effects. The first is that it takes extra work to overcome friction and make things move. As a result, machines use more power and are less efficient if there is a lot of friction between their moving parts. Secondly, heat is produced as things rub together. (You can feel this for yourself if you rub your hands together vigorously.) Inside

Above: *Tread like this, on the surface of tires, increases friction between the tire and the road and so prevents vehicles from slipping or skidding. Tractors and earth movers which work in very muddy, slippery conditions have particularly deep treads on their tires. When there is ice and snow on the road, some people fit special chains, called snow chains, around their tires to increase grip even more.*

Professional skiers like the woman in the photograph on the left often grease the undersides of their skis to reduce friction between the skis and the snow. The greased skis can travel more quickly over the snow.

an engine, frictional heat can damage moving parts and make the engine seize up. To reduce friction, engines, wheels and many other things with moving parts are lubricated with oil. This separates the parts by forming a thin layer between them. A lubricated engine works for longer because the moving parts remain in good order and the reduced friction means it uses less energy.

Reducing friction by smoothing out uneven surfaces, or by greasing and polishing, are other ways to make things run more easily and quickly. Fast-moving cars and aircraft have sleek, smooth shapes to reduce friction between their bodies and the air, and the fastest slide is the one with the most polished surface therefore presenting least friction.

Above: *Skaters slide easily over ice because, where the blades of their skates meet the ice, the skaters' weight causes enough pressure to melt a small amount of ice. The thin layer of water that is produced acts as a lubricant between the skates and the ice.*
Left: *Investigate friction by sliding various objects of roughly the same size, but with different surface textures, down a sloping wooden bread board or a metal tray. Some objects move more easily than others because there is less friction between their surface and the slope.*

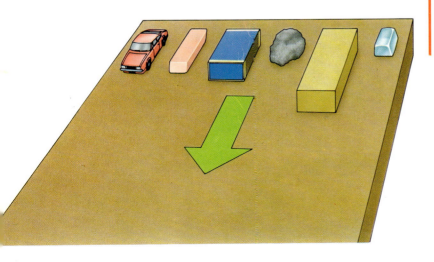

Before the invention of the wheel, people used rollers to move loads. The simple cart shown below is from Sumeria (Iraq), about 5,000 years ago. Its solid wheels are made from sections of tree trunks. The diagram on the far left, below, shows how these wheels fitted onto the cart.

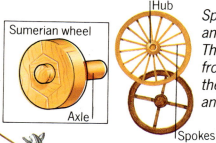

Sumerian wheel
Hub
Axle
Spokes

Spoked wheels were lighter and yet structurally strong. They grew in importance, from Celtic war chariots to the carriages of the 18th and 19th centuries (below).

Right: *The wheel was vital to the start of the Industrial Revolution in the late 1700s. Samuel Crompton's "Spinning Mule" (1779) used wheels to spin different yarns.*

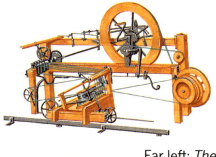

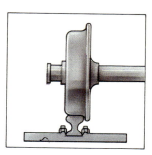

Far left: *The steam engine was discovered in the 1700s and people saw how it could be made to turn wheels—the age of locomotives had begun. Stephenson's "Rocket" started it all. Train wheels are grooved and run along metal rails, as shown left.*

The wheels of modern cars, made of metal with rubber tires, turn as fuel is burned and pistons move up and down in the engine. This "internal combustion" engine could not work without another kind of wheel—a "flywheel" on a shaft that keeps up a smooth flow of energy. Flywheels have been crucial to the course of modern industry.

Left: *Cycling downhill is much faster because gravity is doing most of the work, naturally pulling the cyclist "downward." Racing bicycle tires have fine treads and are pumped to a high pressure. This reduces the amount of contact with the road and so reduces friction. The riders themselves dress in tight-fitting clothes that minimize wind resistance and so increase their speed.*

Rolling along

As long ago as 4000 B.C., the men who built Stonehenge probably used tree trunks as rollers under the huge rocks they moved. They realized that if friction was reduced between a heavy load and rough ground, the load would be easier to push or pull along. No one knows exactly who took the next step and invented the wheel, but in about 3000 B.C. in Asia, people were using carts which had two solid wheels joined together by a pole called an "axle." These early wheels were much more useful than rollers, because the axle could be fitted to the cart and move along with it. Later, in about 1750 B.C., lighter wheels with spokes radiating from a center "hub" were made in Egypt.

Vehicles fitted with early spoked wheels weighed less and moved more quickly. But both solid and spoked wheels turned on a fixed axle and, as they moved, the wheels rubbed against it. The rubbing produced friction, which made it difficult for the wheels to turn and wore them out. Although people greased the wheels, it was not until the 19th century, when "ball bearings" were invented, that the problem was solved. Ball bearings are small steel balls which fit between the center hub of a wheel and the axle, reducing friction.

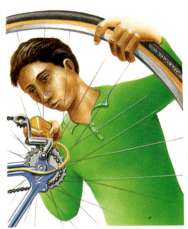

Above: *Bicycles have ball bearings in the wheels, pedals, and steering columns. Each set of bearings is enclosed in a channel called a ball race. Lubricating the bearings keeps the balls turning so the wheel can spin.*

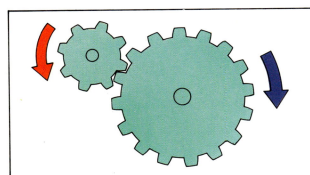

IN GEAR

Gears are toothed wheels that fit together. Each time the large wheel with many teeth rotates, it turns the smaller one with half the teeth twice. Bicycles have gears that link the pedals with the wheels.

7. Electricity and Magnetism

Electricity lights our homes, cooks our food, makes our televisions and radios work, and does thousands of other jobs. But what is it?

Electricity is an invisible form of energy that is stored in electrons and protons—the tiny particles inside atoms. Electrons have a negative electric charge, protons have an equal positive charge. In normal atoms there is an equal number of electrons and protons, so there is an equal amount of negative and positive electricity. To make electricity we must create a situation in which there are more negative or more positive electrons in something and so create an imbalance.

Static and current electricity

There are two forms of electricity—**static** and **current**. "Static" means "stationary." In static electricity the electrons are not moving. In current electricity the electrons are in motion (see diagram on page 62).

Below: *As the balloon on the left is rubbed with the cloth, large areas of their surfaces come into contact. Electrons move from the cloth to the balloon, making the balloon negatively charged and leaving the cloth positively charged. Like charges repel one another, so if two rubbed balloons are held close together they will push each other apart. Unlike charges attract however, so the negatively charged balloon will pick up little bits of positively charged paper.*

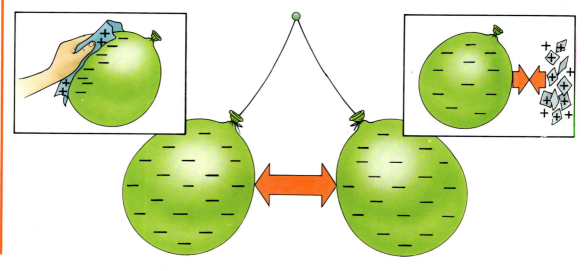

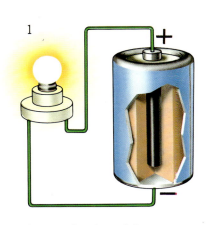

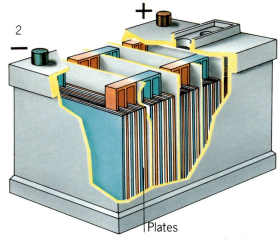

Plates

To make static electricity, run a comb through your hair a few times. Your comb will now attract small pieces of paper. As the comb passes through your hair, some of the comb's electrons are left behind in the hair. Your hair gains electrons, so it gains a negative charge. The comb loses electrons, so it becomes positively charged. Two negative charges—or two positive charges—push each other apart. But opposite charges—a negative and a positive —attract each other. The positively charged comb attracts the electrons in the pieces of paper.

Current electricity is a more controlled flow of electrons that can be produced by a battery or by a machine called a generator (see pages 66–67). Batteries produce a flow of electrons by chemical reactions. The batteries that we use in toys, torches, and radios are "dry" batteries that have an outer case made of zinc. Inside the case, a layer of manganese dioxide surrounds a carbon rod. The rest of the space is filled with ammonium chloride. The zinc, carbon and ammonium chloride react together to produce electricity. The manganese dioxide absorbs hydrogen formed as a by-product. Dry batteries must be thrown away when their chemicals are exhausted and they produce no more electricity.

Above: *1. This "dry" battery and the bulb together make up a "circuit." Current is said to flow from the positive "terminal" to the negative one. 2. A car battery is a "wet" battery because inside, alternate plates of lead and lead oxide are suspended in weak sulfuric acid. The lead plates are connected together to form the negative terminal and the lead oxide ones to form the positive one. Electricity is produced when the plates and acid react.*

Below: *In electrolysis, current passed through a liquid causes a chemical reaction. This can be used in "electroplating."*

Above: *Articles being lifted from an electroplating "bath."*

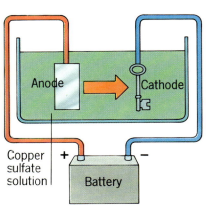

Anode → Cathode

Copper sulfate solution

+ − Battery

ELECTROPLATING

Left: The "anode" here is a copper plate attached to the positive terminal of a battery or generator. The "cathode" is a key attached to the negative terminal. The anode and the cathode are suspended in copper sulfate solution. Copper ions from the anode are attracted to the cathode, coating the key with copper.

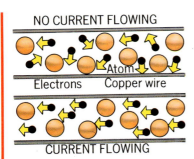

Atom
Electrons Copper wire
CURRENT FLOWING

Above: *Current flows along an ordinary copper wire when electrons from the atoms of the metal move from the negative terminal to the positive terminal of a battery.*

How current electricity flows

Current electricity moves through substances called **conductors**. Conductors conduct electricity because they contain "free" electrons—electrons that are free to move from atom to atom. Most metals have lots of free electrons, so they are good conductors. Silver and copper are the best conductors and so are used to make wires and electrical connections. Other substances have very few free electrons. Few electrons can move from atom to atom, so an electric current cannot flow. These substances are called **insulators**. They are used to cover wires and protect us from electric shocks. Air, glass, rubber, and most plastics are insulators.

Under pressure

Electric current flowing around a circuit is rather like water flowing along a system of pipes. A pump can be used to produce the pressure to push water along, while a battery or generator produces the electrical pressure that causes a current of electricity. Electrical pressure is measured in **volts**. A dry battery produces about 1.5 volts of electricity. As the voltage increases, so does the amount of current that flows. We measure the actual current in units called "amperes" or **amps** for short.

Putting up a resistance

In a pipe full of water, the flow is slowed down because of friction between the water and the sides of the pipe. Similarly, electric current is reduced as moving electrons bump into other electrons or atoms and we say that there is **resistance** to the flow. Conductors allow electricity to flow with little resistance.

Fuses

A fuse is a safety device that is included as part of many circuits. Electrical appliances can be damaged if too great a current flows through them. Some fuses are made of thin wire which gets hot and melts if the current gets above a certain level or "rating." When the fuse melts or "blows," the circuit is broken and the flow of electricity stops.

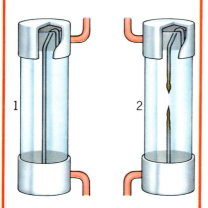

1   2

Above: *1. The cartridge type of fuse that is fitted inside some household plugs. 2. The wire in this fuse has been melted by the frictional heat of too large a current. It will have to be replaced.*

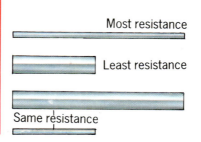

Most resistance

Least resistance

Same resistance

It is easier for electrons to move along a thick wire than to squeeze along a thin one of the same material. We say that the thick wire has a lower "resistance" than the thin one. Also, a current moves more easily along a short wire than a longer one.

Left: *American statesman Benjamin Franklin (1706–90) proved that there was atmospheric electricity by flying a kite in a thunderstorm. Electricity passed from a metal spike on the kite down the string to a metal key, where it produced sparks. He was lucky not to be killed.*

Right: *Italian Luigi Galvani (1737–98) "discovered" electrical current when he used copper hooks to hang frogs' legs from iron bars. The metals and the liquid in the legs produced the same effect as the parts of a battery, and the legs twitched.*

Voltaic pile

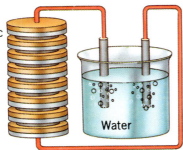

Water

Left: *Italian Alessandro Volta (1745–1827), whose "voltaic pile" was the first battery. Cloth soaked in salt solution was sandwiched between alternate zinc and copper disks. He made the key discovery that current could break water down into hydrogen and oxygen.*

Right: *André Ampère (1775–1836) saw the Dane Hans Oersted show how a current-carrying wire creates a magnetic field that a compass needle will line up with. Ampère showed that electricity could make magnets.*

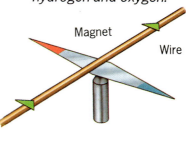

Magnet

Wire

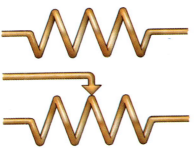

Left: *German George Ohm (1789–1854) discovered that the amount of current flowing in a wire increases as the voltage increases. His law states that resistance equals voltage divided by current.*

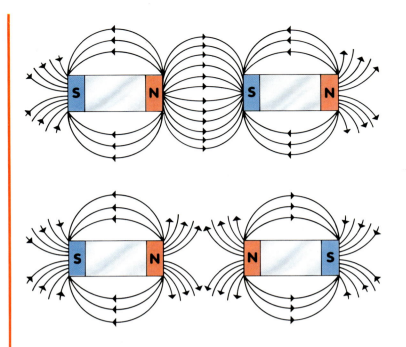

Left: *Magnets exert invisible forces through their poles. The lines of force of their magnetic fields can be "seen" if iron filings are sprinkled on a piece of card resting on top of the magnets. The lines of force show clearly that like poles attract each other and unlike poles repel each other.*

Magical magnets

A magnet can exert a most unusual force. It will overcome gravity and lift small nails and paper clips, it will stick to other magnets, but it will have no effect on things made of wood, plastic, or metals such as silver or copper. In addition, a magnet can pass these unusual properties on to certain other objects. An iron nail which is stroked with a strong magnet will itself become a magnet.

Magnets are made of iron or steel (steel is an alloy that contains a lot of iron). They can only attract or move things made of iron, cobalt, nickel or steel, so we say that these metals are magnetic. But a magnet's influence is limited to the area immediately around it. Only objects within this invisible force field, which we call a **magnetic field**, can be affected. The field spreads out in lines of magnetic force from the ends of the magnet. Farther out from a magnet its field becomes weaker, although magnetic fields can pass through substances such as water and paper without losing their power.

We call the ends of a magnet the **poles**. One is the "north" pole and the other the "south" pole. Two magnets held with like poles facing will be pushed apart by their magnetic fields, while a north pole of one magnet will be attracted to the south pole of another. If any magnet is suspended in the air so that it can turn freely, it will always line up with its north pole pointing in a northerly direction. Magnets behave in this way because the earth has a magnetic field all around it. It is as though there is a huge magnet deep inside the earth with its north pole just below

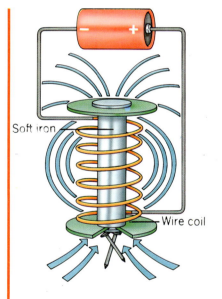

Soft iron

Wire coil

Above: *A wire coil is wrapped around a soft iron bar and connected to a battery. While current flows, the iron bar becomes an electromagnet and attracts metal pins and paper clips. The magnet could be made stronger by making more turns in the wire or by passing a stronger current through the wire coil.*

Because electromagnets attract iron and steel they can be used to lift heavy pieces of these metals. This photograph shows sets of lifting magnets being used to move sheets of steel. The magnets are suspended from a beam that is controlled by a crane. The crane operator can control each set of magnets.

Antarctica and its south pole near the earth's North Pole. Any magnet suspended in the field of this giant imaginary magnet will line itself up along the lines of magnetic force.

From electricity to magnetism

In 1820, a Danish scientist called Hans Oersted noticed that when electric current was flowing along a wire, it produced a magnetic field around the wire. This magnetism produced by an electric current is called **electromagnetism**.

If wire is wound around and around to form a coil, and an electrical current is passed through the wire, one end of the coil becomes a north pole and the other a south pole while the current flows. The strength of the magnetism increases if the wire is wound around a core of metal. If the core is made of steel, the steel will become permanently magnetized by the current. But if soft iron is used, the metal is magnetized only while the current is switched on.

Below: *This box shows an ordinary compass, used for navigation. A compass needle is a small magnet that always lines up with the earth's magnetic field. Among the first to use magnets for navigation were Chinese sailors of the 12th century. They suspended "lodestones"—pieces of a magnetic rock and used them as simple compasses.*

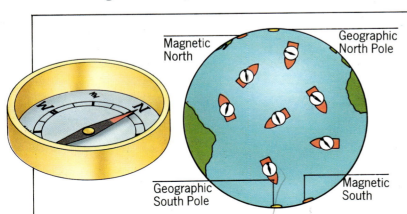

Magnetic North

Geographic North Pole

Geographic South Pole

Magnetic South

WHICH POLE?

The earth's magnetic field does not line up exactly with the geographic Poles, so a compass does not point directly at the North Pole. This difference is called the "magnetic variation."

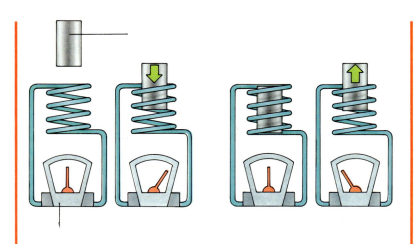

From magnetism to electricity

After the discovery that electricity could produce magnetism, scientists began to wonder whether the reverse might be possible—could magnetism be used to make electricity? In 1830, a British scientist called Michael Faraday began a series of experiments with magnets and coils of wire. He found that current was produced in a coil of wire when a magnet was moved in and out of it. This discovery was of great importance. What Faraday had found was a way to turn mechanical energy, the movement of the magnet, into electrical energy. The faster the magnet was moved in and out of the coil, the greater the current it produced. Current flowed first one way and then the other to give an **alternating current—AC**. Later, a mechanical engine was used to move the magnet and the first simple electricity generator had been made.

Generators

The current produced in such a generator is made by the wire passing through the magnet's field. But the same effect can be obtained, as Faraday later discovered, if a wire is moved through the magnetic field of a stationary magnet. Modern generators are made like this, because wires are easier to move than magnets.

Inside a generator, a coil of wire is turned between the poles of a magnet. Half way through each turn, the coil

Left: *One of Faraday's experiments, using a wire coil attached to a device that detects current (galvanometer) and a magnet.*

When the magnet is out of the coil (1), no current flows, so the pointer does not register anything—it stays in the middle. Moving the magnet into the coil (2) causes current to flow and the pointer swings to the right. When the magnet is stationery inside the coil (3), the pointer does not move. Pulling the magnet out (4) makes the pointer move to the left. Current flows only when the magnet is moving and its direction depends on the direction in which the magnet moves.

Below: *An AC and a DC generator. Inside both, a wire coil is held between the poles of a magnet. Electricity is produced when the coil turns in the magnetic field. The magnetic force makes electrons in the wire move. An AC generator is joined to the rest of the circuit by a slip ring and carbon brushes. The DC one has a commutator instead.*

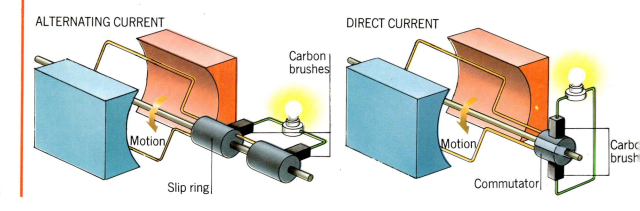

ALTERNATING CURRENT

DIRECT CURRENT

Carbon brushes

Motion

Slip ring

Motion

Commutator

Carbon brush

Above: *Part of the turbine hall that houses the huge turbines and generators in a power station. The bladed wheels of the turbines rotate and turn the coils inside the generators.*

In a simple motor, like the one below, a coil of wire is held between the two poles of a magnet. Electric current from the battery turns the coil into an electromagnet. The poles of the ordinary magnet repel the electromagnet, forcing it to spin around.

becomes positioned, for an instant, at right angles to the magnet. This causes the direction of the current being produced by the generator to change. This AC can be shown as a graph which has the shape of a wave (see page 69). The first half of a revolution produces current in one direction and the second half in the other. The current varies from zero to a maximum or minimum and back again.

Direct current—DC, similar to that from a battery, can be obtained from a generator by using a device called a "commutator." This makes the current flow continuously in the same direction, without reversing as AC does.

Motors

As Faraday continued with his experiments, he found that a wire suspended in a magnetic field would move if a current was passed through it. This was exactly the opposite to what happened in a generator. The movement was caused by a combination of the forces from the magnet and the electric current. Faraday had established the principles on which electric motors work.

Electric motors are machines that make electricity do work, such as turning wheels. They are built in much the same way as generators and work as electric current flows through coils suspended between the poles of a magnet. If the electricity supply is AC, it must be passed through a commutator so that the current flows and the motor turns in one direction only.

One great advantage of electric motors is their flexibility. They can be made small enough to run a hair drier or large enough to drive industrial machines. Motors have not just one coil of wire, but a whole series of coils to give a smooth turning movement. Some motors run on AC supplied from the mains, while others use DC from a battery. Electric motors are also clean and don't produce exhaust fumes. In the future, we may travel in electric cars if we can make an efficient light-weight battery. This problem may be solved by solar batteries that get their power from the Sun (see page 119).

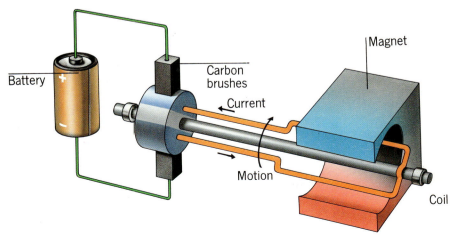

Battery

Carbon brushes

Current

Motion

Magnet

Coil

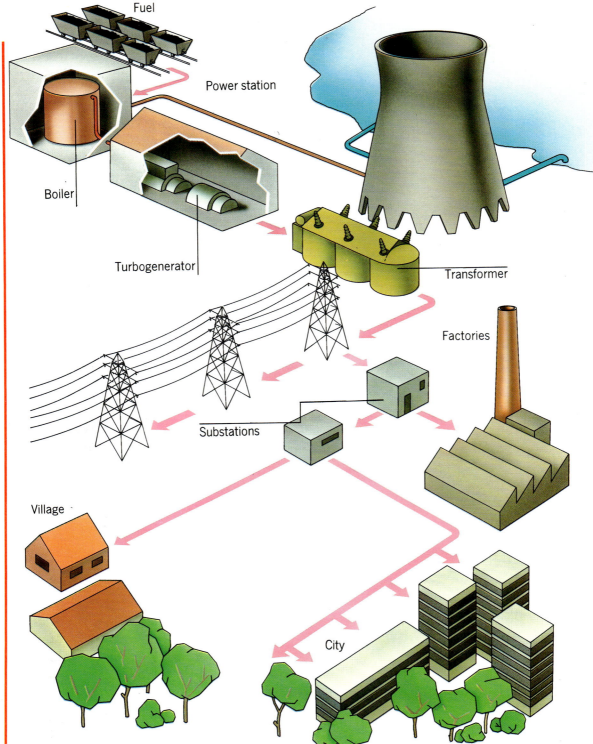

Fuel

Power station

Boiler

Turbogenerator

Transformer

Factories

Substations

Village

City

Getting power to your home

Just as chemical energy can be turned into electricity in a battery, so the same conversion on a huge scale can supply the electricity we need in our homes and factories. Today, we get the energy we need to make electricity from a number of sources of stored energy. Currently the most

The picture above traces the route of electricity from a power station, along overhead cables to sub-stations and from there via underground cables or overhead lines to our homes and factories.

important of these is coal, although nuclear fuels, oil and hydroelectric power (all explained elsewhere in the book) are other important sources.

Electricity is produced in power stations where the fuel is used to heat water in huge boilers several yards high. Steam from the boilers turns large, bladed wheels called "turbines." Each turbine is coupled to a generator to form a turbogenerator. As the turbine rotates, it turns the rotor (the coil and central shaft—see page 67) of the generator and alternating current is produced. A transformer (see below) at the power station increases the voltage of the electricity and it is transmitted through overhead power lines and underground cables to our homes.

As the electricity travels, some of its power is lost through cables and connections, even although they are all well insulated. By increasing the voltage, these losses can be reduced, so "high-voltage" cables you can see on tall pylons each carry up to a massive 400 kilovolts (a kilovolt is 1,000 volts) of electricity. Before it reaches our homes, this voltage is reduced by "step-down" transformers at the local substation. In every house, electricity passes through a meter before it is used. Meters measure the amount of power that each home uses. Most electrical equipment, from light bulbs to power tools, is marked with the voltage it uses and its power rating in watts. (A watt is a unit of electrical power, equal to voltage times current.)

Controlling the supply

Large power stations work night and day. Each one supplies thousands of kilowatts of power, but the amount of electricity needed varies according to the time of day and the season. To ensure that electricity is distributed evenly and that there is always a sufficient supply, all power stations are linked to a country-wide network of cables.

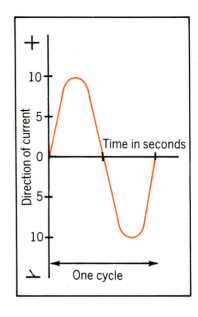

Above: *This graph shows how alternating current changes all the time building up to a maximum in one direction, going back to zero, and then reversing. The number of whole cycles each second gives the frequency.*

The box below shows transformers. These are used to increase or decrease AC voltage. They work by "electromagnetic induction" (see Faraday's experiment on page 66).

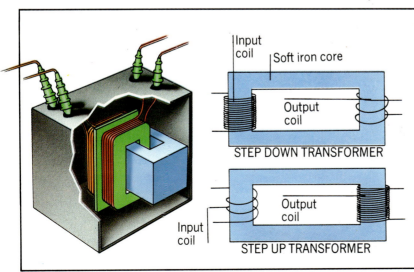

Input coil
Soft iron core
Output coil
STEP DOWN TRANSFORMER

Output coil
Input coil
STEP UP TRANSFORMER

UP AND DOWN

Current passed through the "input" coil produces a magnetic field. This produces current in the "output" coil. To "step up" (increase) voltage, the output coil must have more turns than the input. To "step down" (reduce) voltage, it must have fewer turns.

8. Chemistry

Chemists investigate the properties and structure of all the matter that makes up the earth and the universe. They also study the way in which different substances react together, and how new substances are made. Two thousand years ago, the famous Greek philosopher Aristotle thought that all things were made of just four substances—earth, fire, water, and air. It is only in the last two hundred years that chemists have discovered that there are just over one hundred different **elements** making up all known substances. We call something an element if it cannot be split up into a simpler substance (see page 16).

Inside elements

In 1803, John Dalton explained that all elements are made up of tiny particles called **atoms** which he thought could not be divided into smaller parts. It was not until the end of the nineteenth century that two scientists, Sir Joseph

Below: *This painting by Joseph Wright shows an alchemist at work with his assistants. Alchemy was a strange mixture of astrology, science, and religion. The people who practiced it dreamed of producing a substance they called the "philosopher's stone" which could change metals such as lead into gold. Philosopher's stone was never found but alchemists did devise one of the first series of symbols to represent metals.*

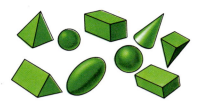

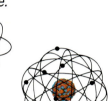

Right: *John Dalton imagined that there were just a few basic types of atom, each made of a different substance.*

Left: *Democritus, a Greek scholar who lived around 500B.C. believed that matter was made of differently shaped atoms made of the same substance.*

Left: *In 1911 Lord Rutherford showed that atoms of different elements have different numbers of electrons that orbit around a nucleus.*

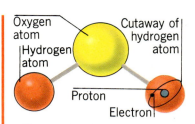

Above: *A water molecule with a hydrogen atom cut away. A hydrogen atom is very simple—just one electron orbiting a nucleus of one proton (no neutrons).*

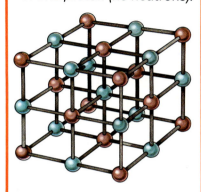

Above: *A model of a sodium chloride molecule. Sodium and chlorine atoms are linked to form a very regular square lattice.*

Thomson and Lord Rutherford, discovered that atoms are made up of even smaller particles called **protons**, **neutrons**, and **electrons**. However, an atom is the smallest particle that can take part in a chemical change.

Protons and neutrons are bound together at the **nucleus** (center) of an atom. Electrons orbit around the nucleus. Usually an atom has the same number of electrons as protons. Protons have a positive charge, which cancels out the negative charge of the electrons. If the balance of electrons and protons is upset by adding or removing electrons, the atom becomes either negatively or positively charged. Charged atoms are called **ions**. Groups of atoms, joined together by chemical bonds, are called **molecules** (see page 16). If all the atoms in a molecule are alike they form an element, if different elements are combined they form a **compound**.

Below: *In a molecule, the bonds that join atoms are formed from atoms "sharing" electrons. Here, a sodium atom and a chlorine atom share an eighth electron, to form a molecule of sodium chloride.*

Naming the elements
Chemists use a simple shorthand system to refer to the atoms of various elements. The system used now was invented by the Swedish chemist J. J. Berzelius in 1813. It uses the first letter of the English or Latin name of each element to represent an atom of that element. So the symbol for carbon is C, phosphorus is P, oxygen is O, and so on. If two elements have the same initial letter, then a second letter is added—manganese is written as Mn and magnesium is Mg. Compounds are represented by combinations of the appropriate letters, CO_2 is the gas carbon dioxide—one atom of carbon combined with two of oxygen; calcium chloride is $CaCl_2$ and so on.

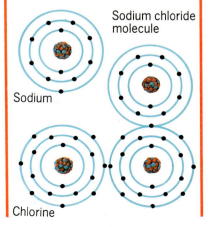

Sodium chloride molecule

Sodium

Chlorine

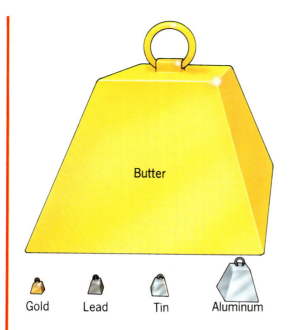

Butter

Gold   Lead   Tin   Aluminum

Left: *Metals have very high densities. Just a tiny piece of gold weighs the same as a large lump of butter. Aluminum is one of the lighter metals but even aluminum is more dense than butter.*

Above: *Heat is carried easily through metal objects. The handle of a metal spoon in a hot drink will get hot, while the plastic one remains cool.*

Metals

It is not easy to say exactly what a metal is. Most metals conduct heat and electricity well. Many of them are shiny, and they can usually be beaten into shapes or drawn out into wire. The only metal that is a liquid at ordinary temperatures is mercury.

Precious metals

Gold and silver are probably the most valued—"precious" —metals. Gold is valuable not only because it is rare —only about 80,000 tons of gold have been mined since 4000 B.C.—but also because it is useful. Gold does not react with other substances, so it does not rust or tarnish. Only the strongest acid will dissolve it. These properties make gold useful as a corrosion-proof covering for parts of satellites and aircraft.

Gold conducts electricity so well, and is so resistant to decay, that it is used to make connections in computers. Silver is a metal that conducts electricity better than any other. This is because its atoms are arranged in very regular patterns which do not impede the flow of electrons. However, the metal copper is also a very good conductor, and because it is so much cheaper than gold or silver, it is usually used to make electrical wires.

Mixing metals

Gold, copper, and silver are three metals that we often use in their pure form. Mixing one metal with another metal or with a non-metal produces **alloys**. These can have very useful properties. For example, a major use of gold is in

Below: *Applying a thin sheet of gold called "gold leaf" to an antique chair. Gold is the most malleable metal known. An ounce of gold can be beaten into a sheet 12 square yards in area.*

Above: *Bronze, an alloy of tin and copper, has been used for many centuries. These bronze-tipped spears are nearly 2,000 years old and the bronze vessel was made in China in about 1100 B.C. Alloys are usually made by "smelting," where two or more metals are heated until they melt. The liquids are then mixed together and cooled.*
Above right: *The George Washington Bridge, New York. It is made of steel— an alloy of iron, carbon, and other metals (see next page). The bridge can support several lanes of heavy traffic.*

jewelry, but pure gold is too soft for this and so it is mixed with small amounts of other metals.

Alloys also have more practical uses. Duralumin—a mixture of aluminum and magnesium—is strong and light. This makes it ideal for constructing aircraft and high-speed trains. Lithium, the lightest metal, is used in alloys for similar purposes. Tungsten, osmium, and iridium are the three heaviest metals. Tungsten is so hard that it is used to make the tips of high-speed drills, while alloys of iridium are made into styli for record players, pen nibs and spark plugs for aircraft. Osmium is the hardest and heaviest of all, a piece of it the size of a brick weighs an incredible 55 pounds.

LIQUID METALS

Not all metals are solid at ordinary temperatures. Mercury is a liquid metal. Like all metals, it expands (increases in volume) when heated. Mercury used in a thermometer is enclosed in a glass tube. As the temperature increases, it expands and rises up the tube. Mercury forms alloys with most metals. Dentists' "amalgam"—mercury mixed with other metals—is used to fill teeth.

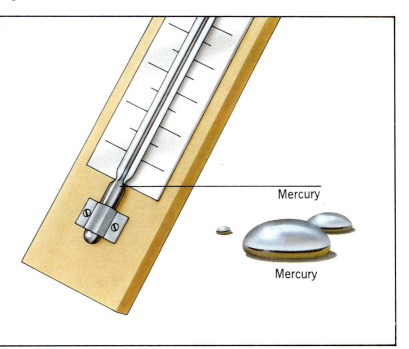

Mercury

Mercury

Iron and steel

Iron and steel are two substances that we use in very large quantities. In the U.S.A., more than 100 million tons of steel are made every year. Steel is an alloy of iron with carbon and one of a number of other metals which include manganese, chromium, and nickel. By adding these metals, steel can be made that is suitable for almost any purpose from knives and forks to cars, buses, and girders.

Iron, like most metals, is found in the ground combined with other elements, in the form of an "ore." Oxides of iron are the ores used in steelmaking. The first step is to extract iron from the ore by "smelting." The smelting process heats the ore to a very high temperature and turns the iron in the ore into liquid metal.

Smelting takes place in huge "blast furnaces" up to 100 feet high and 30 feet across at the base. Iron ore is mixed with coke and limestone and as the furnace is heated, carbon from the coke combines with the oxygen of the ore, leaving the iron behind. Limestone combines with other minerals in the ore and forms a liquid called "slag." Blasts of very hot air give the furnace its name and make it so hot that most of the impurities are burned away. Before it is blown in, this air is heated in hot blast stoves almost as big as the furnace. Liquids extracted from the ore gather at the bottom of the furnace in a brick-lined tank called the hearth. Slag floats on the top and liquid iron collects at the bottom.

Below: *This diagram shows how iron is made in a blast furnace. Iron ore, limestone, and coke (made from coal), are unloaded from skips into the top of the blast furnace. As the furnace is heated, molten metal and slag collect at the bottom. The blast stove is used to warm air up before it is blasted into the furnace. As the furnace operates, waste gases escape from the top of it. These are collected and any impurities in the gases are removed in the dust catcher and spray chamber. Clean gases are taken away and stored. Later they will be burned and used to heat the furnace.*

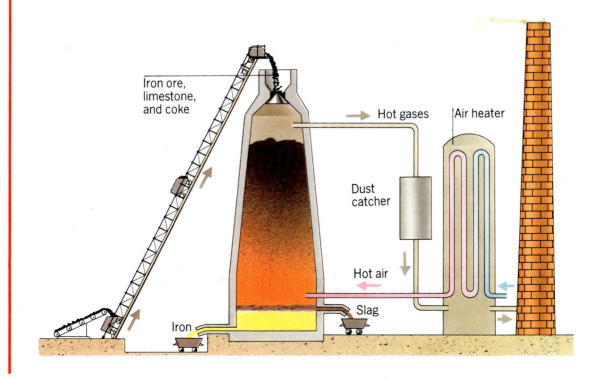

Iron ore, limestone, and coke

Hot gases

Air heater

Dust catcher

Hot air

Slag

Iron

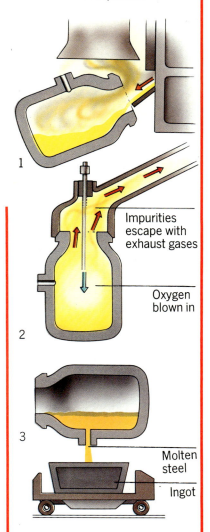

Impurities escape with exhaust gases

Oxygen blown in

Molten steel

Ingot

Liquid iron can be cast into many shapes in wooden molds lined with heat-resisting sand. But cast iron, despite being strong and hard, cannot be bent into shape—it is brittle and snaps. So, a good deal of the liquid iron from a blast furnace is kept molten and turned into steel in a process described below.

Steel

Steel-making takes out some of the carbon that the liquid iron contains, and adds other metals to make an alloy. Most steel is made by a process called "oxygen steel-making." Molten iron is poured from enormous ladles, which can hold up to 100 tons, into a simple furnace—a large steel vessel lined with heat resistant bricks. Scrap metal and other ingredients may be added and then oxygen, or an air and oxygen mixture, is blown straight down onto the metal. Any carbon in the metal burns out in this oxygen. A typical steel-making furnace can convert 180 tons of hot metal into steel in just 20 minutes.

Steel can be shaped either by casting it in molds or by pouring it into blocks called "ingots" which are sent to be rolled into thin sheets. Cast steel makes many objects from engines to bulldozer parts, while rolled steel sheets are used for shipbuilding, cars, and cans. Some steel is drawn out into rods, wire beams, and girders at specialized rolling mills.

Steel products can be protected in a number of ways to make them last longer. Sheet steel is often "galvanized" (coated) with zinc to make it rustproof. If it is to be used to make cans, it may be coated with tin, which gives it resistance to the acids in food and fruits. Steel used for furniture is often coated with plastic, and steel pans are "enamelled"—given a special coating that looks like enamel—that makes them more attractive and also increases their durability.

Most steel we use today is made by the "Linz-Donawitz" method shown here. 1. The furnace is "charged" (filled) with about 50 tons of scrap iron and 120 tons of molten iron. 2. The furnace is tilted upright and has oxygen blown into it. This produces enough heat to burn out impurities. After about 20 minutes, molten steel can be poured from the furnace into ingots (3).

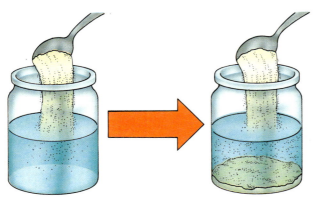

Mixing and dissolving

If a spoonful of sugar is added to a glass of water, the crystals soon disappear completely and we say that the sugar has dissolved. The sugar forms a **solution** with the water, but we know that it is still there by the sweet taste of the liquid. The molecules of sugar have not been chemically changed as they dissolved, they have simply spread out and fitted in between the molecules of the water. If several more spoonfuls are added, they too will dissolve. But eventually the water will hold no more and crystals of undissolved sugar will sink to the bottom of the glass. There are no more spaces in the liquid, which has become a "saturated" solution.

Not all substances will dissolve in water. Some mix in, but their physical form remains unchanged. Powdered chalk behaves like this—when mixed with water its particles stay floating in the liquid for a short time to produce a milky **mixture** called a "suspension."

Colloids are a special type of solution. Particles dispersed in a colloid are intermediate in size—not small enough to disappear completely, but large enough to remain suspended in the liquid without sinking immediately. A colloid made in water is given the name "emulsion." Paints are emulsions and so is milk, which is an emulsion of fat in water. A small amount of oil shaken in water also forms an emulsion, but small drops of oil soon separate from it. If a little soapy detergent is added, the mixture lasts much longer without separating.

Left: *One teaspoon of sugar dissolves in the water to form a sugar solution. When much more sugar is added, some sinks to the bottom, because the solution is saturated.* Below: *Many medicines are suspensions of substances in liquid that settle into layers. We must "Shake the bottle" to remix the contents.*

Below: *A simple experiment with colloids. 1. Add a little cooking oil to water. The two substances settle into two layers. 2. When the jar is shaken, the water and oil almost mix, but soon settle back into layers. 3. A few drops of liquid soap are added. 4. The detergent breaks up the drops of oil and a lasting colloid is produced. Detergent is used for washing because it brings grease into a colloidal solution that will rinse away.*

Water
Oil

Detergent

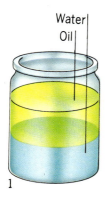

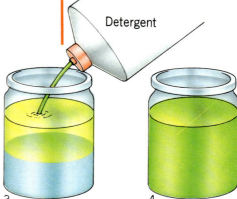

1   2   3   4

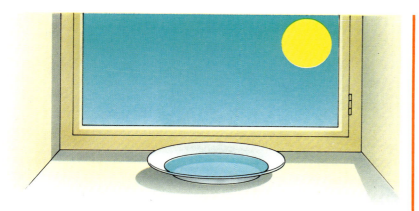

Left: *A saucer of salty water left on a sunny windowsill will soon evaporate and leave crystals of salt behind. Water also evaporates from many other places, for example from wet washing and from rain puddles on the ground. The evaporating water becomes part of the water cycle (see page 9).*

Solids from liquids

Substances mixed with liquids to form suspensions or solutions may be changed in appearance but their chemical structure is not changed. So, we can collect either the substances or the liquids without any chemical reaction taking place.

A mixture such as chalk and water can be separated easily by pouring the suspension through a filter paper. Filter paper is a special unglazed paper which has many tiny holes in it. Water passes easily through the holes and can be collected underneath, but chalk particles are too large to go through the holes and stay trapped on the paper. Filtering will remove most solids from their mixtures but cannot separate dissolved substances from solutions because there are no free, suspended particles to trap.

To collect a solid from a solution, salt from sea water for example, we must use a process called **evaporation**. By warming sea water in a dish we drive off molecules of water as a vapor. As the water dries up—evaporates—crystals of salt begin to form and are left behind in the dish. Evaporation enables us to collect the salt in sea water, but if we wish to collect the water we must use another process called **distillation** (see below).

Below: *This box shows how to make distilled (pure) water. Distillation is the process of turning liquid into vapor, condensing the vapor and collecting the condensed liquid. It is used to separate liquids with different boiling points from a mixture, or to separate a pure liquid from a solution.*

For example, pure water can be collected from sea water or tap water. (Tap water actually contains small amounts of minerals.)

Distillation is also used for producing alcoholic drinks and perfume and for refining crude petroleum.

DISTILLING WATER

Sea water heated in the flask turns to vapor, rises to the top of the flask and into the cold condenser. Cold water circulating around the condenser cools the vapor, which turns back into liquid and collects as distilled water in the beaker.

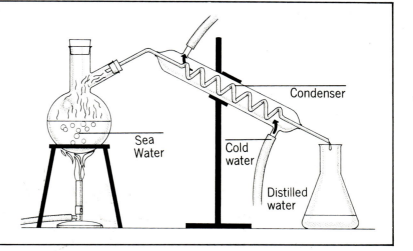

Salt and other crystals

Common salt—scientific name sodium chloride—is one chemical compound that is familiar to almost everyone. We use it as a flavoring for our food and need a certain level of it to keep our muscles and nerves working properly. Salting has been used for hundreds of years as a way to preserve foods such as beef and pork because bacteria cannot survive in high concentrations of salt.

Salt occurs naturally, as deposits of **crystals** in the ground. Where the deposits are pure enough, for instance in Germany, Poland, Siberia in Russia, and Cheshire in England, salt can be mined. In warmer parts of the world, salt is extracted from sea water. Sea water is collected in shallow pools and allowed to evaporate in the sun leaving crystals of salt behind.

Salt dissolves very easily. Up to 2 ounces of salt will dissolve in a 16 cubic inch glass of water, giving a solution of salt water that has quite different properties from pure water. Salt water freezes at a lower temperature than fresh water so, even though the weather may be cold enough to freeze a river, the sea rarely becomes frozen. Grains of salt sprinkled on ice during the winter form a salt solution on the surface of the ice and cause it to melt. This makes salt very useful as a deicer on slippery paths.

Salt water has a greater density than fresh water. This means that things can float more easily on salty water. The greater the amount of salt which is dissolved in water, the greater the density. It is said to be impossible to sink in the Dead Sea—the world's saltiest sea.

Above: *This photograph shows how salt is collected from sea water on the island of Lanzorote. Sea water is channeled into shallow pools and left to evaporate in the heat of the sun. As the salt crystals form they are drawn into piles at the sides of the pools. When the piles are large enough they are taken away by truck.*

Crystals

There are nearly three thousand minerals found on earth. All but a few of these form special shapes called crystals when conditions are suitable. Most naturally-occurring crystals contain combinations of the elements which make up the earth's crust, although a few, such as crystals of gold and silver, are made of just one element.

As a crystal forms, the atoms and molecules within it always line themselves up in the same orderly, symmetrical patterns which build up to make a three dimensional framework called a "lattice." The arrangement of the lattice determines the shape and other properties of a crystal. Crystals occur in a variety of forms, but they can be divided into six groups based on these shapes. The most important feature of any crystal is the angle between its faces. For example, the very regular, cubic crystals of salt have all their faces at 90° to one another (see page 71).

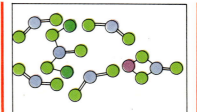

Glass is one clear solid that does not have regular crystals. Its structure is said to be "amorphous" which means shapeless. This diagram shows the arrangement of atoms in glass—there is no set pattern.

Calcite
(hexagonal
system)

Pyrite
(cubic
system)

Gypsum
(monoclinic
system)

Zircon
(tetragonal
system)

Sulfur
(orthorhombic
system)

Rhodonite
(triclinic
system)

Left: *The crystals of water that make snowflakes all have a symmetry based on the number six. Some have six points, others have six sides, but no two flakes are ever exactly the same.*
2. Most of the earth's minerals have regular structures of crystals. There are six main "systems" (types) of mineral crystal shape, based on the size, shape, number, and angle of the faces of each crystal. Examples of some systems are shown here. It is often difficult to pick out the shape of individual crystals, but the different shapes make the general appearance of one type of mineral very different from another.

Crystals everywhere

All rocks are made of crystals of various minerals. Usually the crystals are too small to see and thin slices of rock must be examined under the microscope to reveal them. Quartz is the mineral most often found—it makes up 90 percent of all rocks. Agates found inside many pebbles on the beach are one form of quartz and sand is another. The small grains of sand are actually tiny pieces of quartz that have been worn away from rocks by the action of sea and wind over the years.

The word crystal comes from a Greek word *krystallos*, which means "ice-cold." It was once thought that the clear, transparent shapes of many crystals were caused because they had been frozen. In fact, most minerals develop into crystals as they solidify from gases or liquids. The largest crystals form inside cavities in rocks. Over hundreds of years, water trickling through rock produces mineral-rich liquids, and as the water evaporates, crystals are left behind. The size of individual crystals depends on the speed at which evaporation takes place. The slower the rate of evaporation, the larger the crystals. The largest single crystal ever found was a crystal of the gem stone beryl. It was found on the island of Madagascar in 1976, measured 16 feet in length by more than 36 feet across, and weighed in at a staggering 838,000 pounds!

Above: *Stalactites and stalagmites in a German cave. Sometimes the stalactites grow down to meet the up-growing stalagmites and form strange pillars of rock. Stalactites are formed as rainwater seeps through cracks in the roof of limestone caves. The drops of water are saturated with calcium carbonate. As each drop hangs for a while, some water evaporates, leaving a tiny deposit of calcium carbonate on the cave roof. Very slowly, these deposits grow to form stalactites. Drops reaching the floor of the cave gradually form stalagmites that grow upward.*

GROW YOUR OWN STALAGTITES AND STALAGMITES

1. Fill two jars with warm water. Dissolve as much washing soda (sodium carbonate) as you can in each. 2. Arrange a piece of thick wool so that each end is in solution and the middle is hanging down between the jars over a saucer. 3. Put one crystal of washing soda on the saucer and leave the jars for several days. Solution will drip on the crystal in the saucer forming a column.

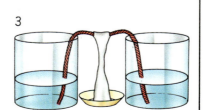

Left: *The difference between a cut and an uncut diamond. Diamonds are cut with delicate saws that are lubricated with diamond dust and oil. Then they are ground and polished so that they may have 58 flat faces (facets). Diamonds sparkle as light is reflected off the insides of the facets.*

Crystal caves

Stalagmites and stalactites are formed in caves by the very slow accumulation of clumps or "aggregates" of calcite (limestone) crystals. The calcite is contained in water which drips through the roof of the cave. Calcite can also be found both as chalk, which does not form crystals, and as marble, which has very regular crystal patterns. Marble is formed when limestone is heated to very high temperatures during volcanic eruptions.

Useful crystals

The crystals of about eighty special minerals are known as "gemstones" because of their beautiful appearance and their value. Many gemstones are used just for making jewelry, while others have less glamorous, but still very important uses as well. The most valuable gemstone is the diamond. A diamond is a crystal of carbon; it is an extremely hard substance that can cut through most materials, including glass. Industrial diamonds are used in the manufacture of drilling and cutting tools, while other stones are used to make styli (plural of stylus) for record players. The finest diamonds are cut and polished for jewelry.

Two more gems that are both attractive and useful are red rubies and blue sapphires. These two gems are both crystals of the same mineral—corundum—but small amounts of metal oxides in them produce two completely different colors. Ruby crystals were the first substances used to make laser beams and sapphires are made into styli which are less expensive than those made of diamonds.

Beryl and quartz are two more minerals that form crystals of different colors. Green emeralds and blue aquamarines are both six-sided crystals of beryl; amethysts and rose quartz are two forms of quartz. Amethysts are colored purple by the presence of a little manganese in their crystals, while rose quartz is a delicate pink color.

Above: *Inside and out. There are many precious stones apart from diamonds and their best-known use is in jewelry. Here, some opals have been made into a magnificent piece of jewelry. Also shown is a detailed X-ray picture of the internal structure of an opal crystal.*

Acids and alkalis

Acid is a word which people often use to mean a corrosive, burning liquid. But only the strongest acids are corrosive. Many others are familiar everyday substances —vinegar is acetic acid, many fruits have citric acid in their juice, and sour milk contains lactic acid. One thing which these and all other weak solutions of acids have in common is a sour taste.

Substances that are the opposite of acids are called **bases**. If acids and bases are mixed together, they form new substances called **salts**. Bases which will dissolve in water form a special group, the **alkalis**. These react with acids to neutralize them, producing a salt and water. Chemists write down such a reaction as a "chemical equation" that looks like this:

$$2NaOH + H_2SO_4 \rightarrow Na_2SO_4 + H_2O$$

Caustic soda —alkali	Sulfuric acid	Sodium sulfate —salt	Water

There are only four common alkalis—caustic soda, caustic potash, ammonia, and slaked lime. In their concentrated forms these substances are dangerous and attack the skin, but in dilute solutions caustic soda and ammonia form part of everyday soaps and cleaning materials and are useful because of their ability to break down oils and fats.

Many vegetable and synthetic dyes are changed in color by acids and alkalis. Try out the effect of acids on beetroot juice, flower petals, or other dyes, by squeezing a few

Above: *The female of some kinds of ants sting, squirting a tiny drop of formic acid into the wound that they make.*

Below: *The devastating effects of "acid rain" on forests. The small picture shows damaged trees. The "acid" is sulfur compounds from industrial smoke dissolved in rain water in the air. This rain often falls hundreds of miles from the factories that gave out the smoke. It falls directly onto leaves, causing damage, and onto the ground, where it gets into roots and harms those.*

drops of lemon juice (citric acid) on to them. Litmus is a special purple dye obtained from lichens (small plants which consist of an alga and a fungus growing together). Litmus is used in laboratories to test whether or not a solution is acidic. Acids turn a litmus solution red, alkalis turn it blue, and substances which are neither acid nor alkaline leave it a purple color. Such substances are said to be neutral.

Everyday acids and alkalis

Both acids and alkalis are very important industrial chemicals. Large amounts of sulfuric acid are used for making fertilizers, for removing rust from metals before they are processed, and for manufacturing dyes and detergents. Sodium hydroxide (caustic soda) is used in making paper, soap, and in the production of aluminum.

On a smaller, domestic scale, the reactions of acids and alkalis are still important to us. Hydrochloric acid helps digest food in our stomachs. If a person produces too much of this he or she will suffer from indigestion and may need to take an antacid (base) tablet to neutralize the acid. Baking powder contains tartaric acid (cream of tartar) and a bicarbonate (base). In water, these two substances react to produce bubbles of carbon dioxide gas. While a cake is baking, these bubbles get trapped inside the cake and make it rise. If you are ever stung by a bee, remember bee stings are acidic and you can ease the pain by neutralizing the acid with the base bicarbonate of soda. But a wasp sting is alkaline so if you are stung, apply a few drops of lemon juice or vinegar both of which are mild acids, and will neutralize the sting.

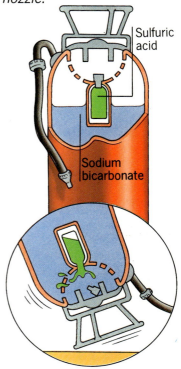

Below: *When this fire extinguisher is turned upside down and banged hard, sulfuric acid mixes and reacts with sodium bicarbonate (an alkali) to produce a build-up of carbon dioxide gas. The gas forces the liquid out of the nozzle.*

Sulfuric acid

Sodium bicarbonate

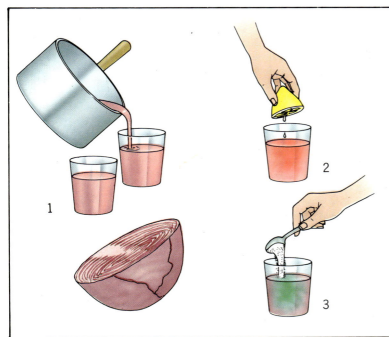

MAKE AN ACID ALKALI INDICATOR

1. Cut half a red cabbage into strips. Put the strips into a bowl, pour hot water on *very* carefully, and let the mixture cool. Strain the liquid into a clean glass. Add a few drops of water to the cabbage solution. This shows the neutral color of the indicator (1). Now add a few drops of lemon juice to show its acid color (2) and some washing soda to show its alkaline color (3).

MARIE AND PIERRE CURIE

Marie and Pierre Curie were French scientists who married in 1895. They were interested in the work of Henri Becquerel who had discovered that the element uranium gives off invisible rays. Marie found that pitchblende—an ore that contains uranium—gave off stronger rays. So she decided to find what was causing the strong rays. The Curies discovered two substances that gave off rays—polonium and radium. They called these elements "radioactive." Marie Curie died in 1934 from leukemia, as a result of handling radioactive materials.

Radioactivity

All elements are made up of atoms. Every atom has a **nucleus**—a small inner core made up of **protons** and **neutrons**. The number of protons in the nucleus of an atom determines what element it is. Around the nucleus circle tiny negative **electrons**. Most atoms are very stable. Strong forces bind the protons and neutrons together in their nuclei (plural of nucleus). But some elements have nuclei that tend to decay, or break apart. We call these **radioactive** elements.

One radioactive element is radium, discovered by Marie and Pierre Curie. When a radium atom decays, it gives off an **alpha particle**—a bundle of two protons and two neutrons. Because it has lost two protons, the atom is no longer an atom of radium. It is now an atom of another element called radon. But radon is radioactive too. After a while the radon atom gives off an alpha particle and becomes a polonium atom.

These three steps—from radium to radon to polonium—are just part of a long chain of radioactive decay that starts with the element uranium and ends up with lead. Ordinary lead is not radioactive, so the decay stops there. Not all of the radioactive elements give off alpha particles. Some of them give off **beta particles**—electrons made in the nucleus of the atom.

The sum of protons and neutrons in an atom is called the element's "mass number." The heavier the element, the greater its mass number. Uranium is the heaviest natural element—it is about two and a half times as heavy as steel. It occurs in several forms, each with a different mass number. Uranium-235 is the one that is most radioactive and is used in atomic bombs and to produce nuclear power. The different kinds of uranium are called **isotopes**. Uranium has 14 isotopes, but only three of them—mass numbers 234, 235, and 238—occur naturally.

Below: *The half life of radioactive iodine-128, a black solid, is only 25 minutes. After 25 minutes, a 16-gram sample of I-28 will contain only 8 grams of the radioactive substance. During the second 25 minutes, it will be reduced to 4 grams, and so on.*

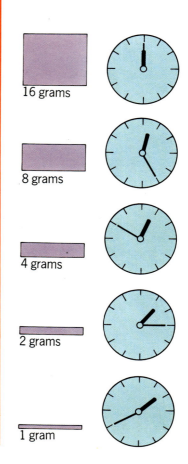

16 grams

8 grams

4 grams

2 grams

1 gram

Half-life

The **half-life** of an isotope is the time it takes for half the atoms to decay to atoms of another element. The half-life of an element may be as short as a fraction of a second or as long as billions of years. The half-life of sodium-24, for example, is 15 hours. During this time half of the atoms in one gram of the substance would decay to atoms of magnesium, leaving half a gram of sodium-24. During the next 15 hours half of the remaining atoms of sodium-24 would decay, leaving one-quarter of the original element, and so on.

Above: *The international symbol for radioactive substances is displayed wherever they are being used or stored.*

Left: *A beta particle is simply an electron expelled by an atom. An alpha particle consists of two neutrons and two protons. The alpha particle is the same as the nucleus of a helium atom.*

Left: *The radioactive series that begins with uranium and ends up with lead, takes millions of years and goes through 15 steps—only a few are shown here. The half-life of uranium-238 is 4,500 million years, which is about the same age as the earth. This means that there was about twice as much U-238 in the earth when it was formed. Half of it has changed into other elements.*

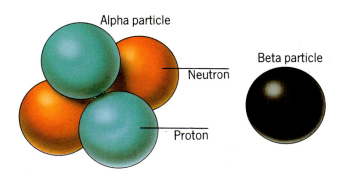

Alpha particle

Neutron

Proton

Beta particle

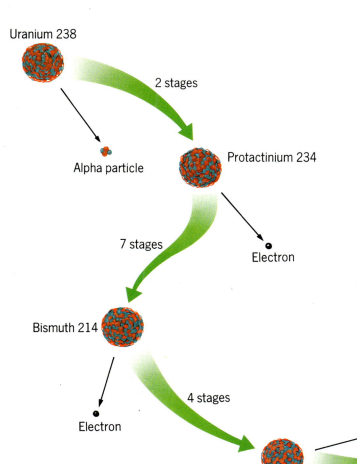

Uranium 238

2 stages

Alpha particle

Protactinium 234

Electron

7 stages

Bismuth 214

Electron

4 stages

Alpha particle

Polonium 214

Lead 206

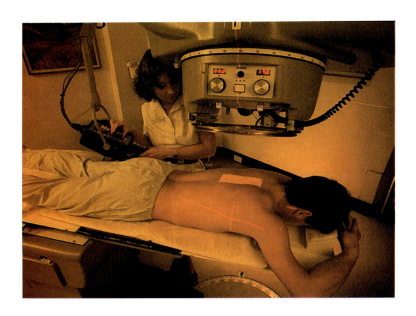

This photograph shows a person being treated by radio therapy. The machine contains radioactive cobalt-60. Gamma rays from the cobalt can penetrate a person's skin and are used to kill cancer cells inside the body. The machine here has been carefully aimed at the target area marked on the patient's back. Gamma rays from the cobalt can be released by opening a shutter in the machine.

Using radioactivity

Several radioactive isotopes occur naturally on earth and because we know that their nuclei disintegrate at a constant rate, we can use them rather like a clock to estimate the age of rock. In the time of a half-life (see page 84), half the original radioactive atoms that were present will have disintegrated. By counting those that remain, the length of time that has passed since the rock was formed can be calculated.

If we say that a piece of uranium ore contained pure U-238 when the Earth was formed, we know that some of it will have decayed, through a number of stages, to lead. So, in any uranium sample, the amount of lead increases as time goes by. The half-life of uranium is 4,500 million years, so if we found an ore with half U-238 and half lead, we would know that the rock was 4,500 million years old. Scientists studying such rock today have used this technique to estimate that the earth is about 5 billion years old.

Another method of estimating ages is called "radiocarbon dating." People, animals, and plants are all slightly radioactive, though not enough to do any harm. They contain a fixed proportion of a radioactive form of carbon called carbon-14, which they take in from the atmosphere. When a person, animal, or plant dies, no more carbon-14 is taken in and the amount left slowly emits beta particles, and decays. Its half-life is 5,570 years. The date when a living thing died can be estimated by measuring the amount of carbon-14 in the remains. If there is only half the proportion found in life, then one half-life has occurred since death and so the remains are 5,570 years old. If only a quarter is left, the age is twice this amount, and so on. Radiocarbon dating can be used to date remains up to about 40,000 years old.

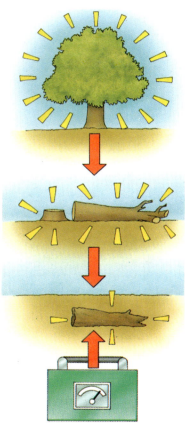

Above: *All living things contain a fixed proportion of radioactive carbon-14. When a tree dies, the amount of carbon-14 left slowly vanishes. The date when the tree died is found by measuring the amount of carbon-14 left in the remains.*

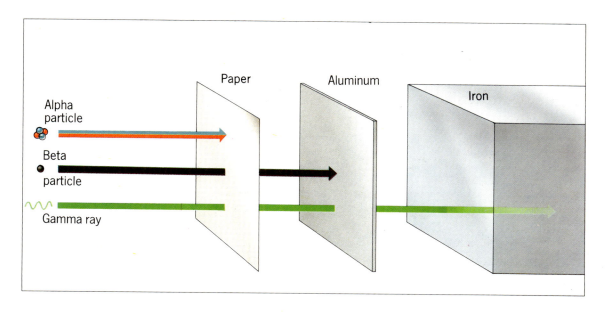

Radioactive isotopes have the same chemical properties as ordinary elements. One of their important uses is as "tracers" in medical diagnosis. For example, a small amount of sodium-24 can be used to study blood circulation. It can be injected into the bloodstream and its course followed with a radiation detector. Only very small amounts are needed and, because the isotope has a short half-life, it soon disappears naturally from the patient's body. Cobalt-60, which gives off penetrating gamma rays, is used to treat cancers. The isotope is contained in a machine that can aim a narrow beam of these rays toward a tumor and kill its cells inside the patient's body. Radioactive isotopes can also be used in engineering to check weldings for faults and to measure the thickness of materials.

Measuring radiation

The device that is most commonly used to detect radiation is the Geiger-Müller tube, otherwise known as the "Geiger counter." A Geiger counter can be designed to detect alpha, beta, or gamma radiation. It contains a tube of gas with a central wire running through the tube. The wire has a positive electric charge. As the radiation particles pass through the gas, they knock electrons from the atoms in the gas. These electrons travel to the wire and produce a signal that is recorded on a meter or as a "click" sound from a loudspeaker.

When a Geiger counter is turned on, it will always record a few counts of radioactivity. These are due to background radiation from cosmic rays and traces of radioactive substances in the air and rocks. The count rate varies over the surface of the earth and it is not constant because radioactive changes take place unpredictably and at random.

Above: The three kinds of radiation have different penetrating powers. An alpha particle can be stopped by a piece of paper. A beta particle is more penetrating, but can be stopped by a thin sheet of aluminum. A gamma ray is very powerful. It can pass through iron 8 inches thick.

Below: Radiation affects the cells of all living things. It can be used to produce new plant types. Here the seedlings of a pink variety of chrysanthemum have been treated with radiation— producing a two-color flower.

9. Energy from the Earth

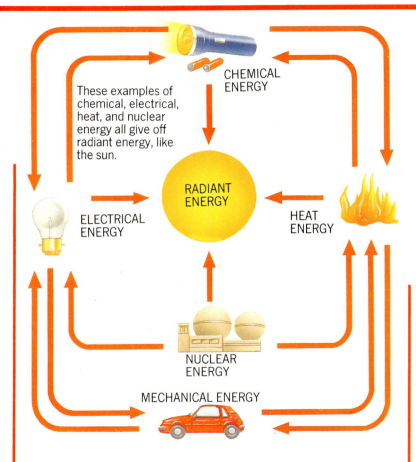

These examples of chemical, electrical, heat, and nuclear energy all give off radiant energy, like the sun.

CHEMICAL ENERGY

RADIANT ENERGY

ELECTRICAL ENERGY

HEAT ENERGY

NUCLEAR ENERGY

MECHANICAL ENERGY

Below: *A pendulum at the top of its swing has potential energy. As it moves, the energy becomes kinetic.*
A moving pool ball has kinetic energy. As it hits another ball, it gives some of its energy to that ball.

Above: *Nearly all the energy on earth has come from the sun. And all forms of energy can be changed into other forms. Every form of energy can be turned into heat.*

It is not easy to explain what energy is. Energy doesn't have a shape like a log of wood or a taste like a bar of chocolate, and yet both these things have energy in them. It is easier to say what energy does—if we burn the wood, its heat energy can keep us warm and if we eat the chocolate, we can use its chemical energy to enable us to run. Energy means being able to do work. The many different forms it takes enable us to do different types of work. Heat and chemical energy are just two forms, others include light, electrical, and mechanical energy.

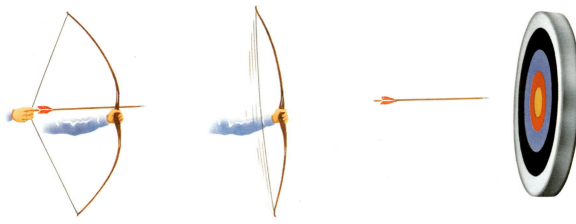

Whatever form energy takes, we can think of it as being in one of two states. **Kinetic** energy is energy that is used for activity or moving. **Potential** energy is stored energy. Usually, a store of potential energy can be released as useful kinetic energy. For example, the wound-up spring in a clockwork toy has potential energy that can become moving kinetic energy and drive the toy.

A hydroelectric power station converts stored potential energy into kinetic, electrical energy that we can use. Water held back behind a dam contains a great deal of energy—it has the potential to turn the turbines in the hydroelectric power station. As water is released from the top of the dam, it falls down and loses its stored energy. As it falls faster and faster, it gains kinetic energy and this energy turns the turbines and generators. The electrical energy they produce can be used to give us heat, light, and sound—all different forms of flowing, kinetic energy.

Running out of energy

You may have heard it said that the world has an "energy crisis." The reason is that our most useful forms of potential energy are fuels like coal, gas, and oil, which will eventually be used up. To solve the problem, we must investigate "renewable" sources of energy, such as solar power and wind power, that will not become exhausted.

Above: *As an archer pulls back a bow, he or she gives it a store of potential energy. When the arrow is released, the potential energy of the bent bow is turned into kinetic (moving) energy. As the arrow hits the target, the energy is used in making a noise and in penetrating the target, while some is lost as heat.*
Below: *This toy travels by using energy stored in a twisted rubber band. If you wind the cotton spool tractor by turning the matchstick, you give it a store of energy. It will drive itself along the floor until the rubber band is unwound and all the potential energy has been used up. You will need a cotton spool, used matchsticks, sticky tape and a rubber band.*

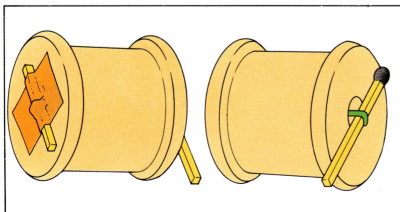

COTTON REEL TRACTOR

Thread the rubber band through the spool. Put half a match through the loop in the band at one end and stick it with tape. Thread another match through the loop at the other end to use as a winder.

Milometer

Passing energy on

The total amount of energy in the universe remains the same because energy cannot be created or destroyed—it can only be changed from one form to another, as we saw on page 88. Heat can be transformed into mechanical energy in a steam engine; chemical energy is released as heat energy when fuel burns; and electrical energy can be converted into sound and light energy, for example in radios and lamps.

The most obvious source of energy on earth is the light and heat we receive from the sun. Although we can collect a little of its energy with solar "cells" (such as those in roof panels—see page 93), we rely on green plants to capture most of the sun's energy for us. Plants are able to capture light in a unique process called "photosynthesis." This turns light energy into stored, chemical energy in the plants' leaves and stems. Life could not exist on Earth without photosynthesis. The stored energy in plants provides the food for every animal and person alive today. If we do not eat the plants themselves, we eat meat from animals that have eaten the plants. As one living thing feeds on another and is itself eaten, a "food chain" is

Above: *Energy from the Sun is captured and stored by plants. This energy forms the first link in the food chain that supplies all animals. As plant-eating animals such as cows and sheep eat grass or leaves, a second link is formed. As we eat meat, milk, or other products from plant-eating animals, yet another link is made in the chain. If someone rides an exercise bicycle, some energy from his food is used. Most is used to move the muscles of his heart, legs, and lungs. Some is converted into the movement of the pedals, which in turn can work a milometer.*

formed, with energy being transferred at each of its links. Animals and people convert the energy from their food into heat and mechanical energy as they live, breathe, and move.

Over millions of years, wood from dead plants has formed our reserves of stored chemical energy in coal, oil, and natural gas (see pages 96–99). These enable us to generate more electrical, mechanical, and heat energy by burning them.

You may wonder why the world is said to have an energy shortage—why can't we continue to turn energy from one form to another if the total amount always remains the same? The answer is that every time energy is converted from one form to another, some of it is always lost as heat. When we use the energy in our muscles to ride a bicycle we get hot; as a car uses energy in gasoline to move, it gets hot, and when coal is burned, it gets hot.

In every process that uses energy, some heat is produced. Most of this heat energy can never be recaptured and changed back to any form that people can use. It is simply wasted as the heat spreads out into the earth's atmosphere. As engines are made more efficient, less energy is wasted.

Left: *Each time you cook a piece of toast you convert electrical energy from the mains supply into heat energy in the elements of the toaster. The heat not only cooks the toast, it also operates a switch in the toaster that makes the toast pop up when it is cooked.*

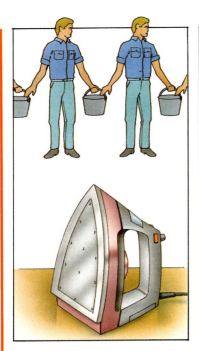

CONDUCTION

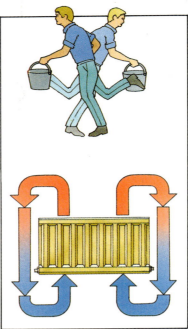

CONVECTION

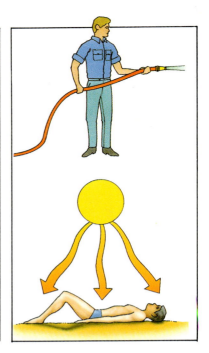

RADIATION

Heat

Energy lost as heat can be moved about—from places where the temperature is higher to those where it is lower. Heat travels in three different ways—by **conduction** through solid materials, by **convection** through liquids and gases, and by **radiation**, through space.

Many solids allow heat to travel right through them by conduction, but the quickest conductors are metals. A running car engine heats up the water inside the car radiator. This in turn heats up the metal of the radiator. But, as heat travels quickly through the metal, it is soon carried away by the air—so the engine does not become overheated.

The opposite of a conductor is an **insulator**. Water, air, glass, rubber, and plastic are insulators and it takes a long time for heat to travel through them. We use insulators to prevent heat from escaping. For example, wearing clothing traps an insulating layer of air between the clothes and our skin, to keep our body heat in.

Heat traveling by convection sets up a movement of air or liquid that is known as a "convection current." Watch a pan of water being heated and you will see ripples rising to the surface. Gases and liquids become lighter when warmed and the ripples are currents of warmed water rising from the bottom of the pan. Cooler water at the top sinks to the bottom, where it is warmed, and so heat moves around the pan. Radiators that warm the air in a room also work on this principle. Hair driers and fan

Above: *The people in these pictures represent the atoms and molecules in heated substances. The water represents heat which is being transferred from place to place. When heat is conducted through the metal of an iron, the metal molecules stay more or less still, just vibrating back and forth as heat is passed from one to the next. This is rather like people passing on buckets of water in a chain. When heat is carried from the radiator by convection, molecules in the air move, taking heat with them. This time the people are carrying buckets of water with them. Heat from the sun travels by radiation—a form of electromagnetic waves. These waves do not need molecules to carry them. The heat travels rather like a continuous stream of water from a hose.*

Left: *White objects reflect most of the light that falls on them. This is why they appear white (see page 31). White things also reflect radiant heat well. Dull black objects absorb light and radiant heat far more than light, shiny ones. The black solar panels on the roof of this house will absorb heat from the sun to provide the house with power, while the white walls will reflect heat and keep the house cool.*

Below: *Nearly every substance expands (increases in size) when it heats up and contracts when it cools. But substances expand by different amounts. This unequal expansion is used to make "thermostats," devices used in refrigerators, electric irons, and heating systems. A thermostat is often a "bimetallic strip," a strip of two different metals bonded together. When the strip heats up it bends because of the unequal expansion of the two metals. As the strip bends, it completes an electrical circuit.*

heaters also work by convection. Air heated by an electric element is blown out of them by a fan. But, because a fan and not just the heat moves the air, this is known as "forced convection."

Radiation—the third method of sending out heat—is probably the most important to us. Heat energy from the sun travels through space to earth by radiation. Radiation or radiant heat, is another name for infrared radiation, a form of electromagnetic waves (see page 42). It travels in straight lines and can be reflected from one object to another. All objects radiate and absorb some heat. If something is hot, it is radiating more heat than it is absorbing. Shiny objects reflect radiant heat well, just as light is reflected from a mirror. The bodies of spacecraft have shiny surfaces to reflect away the fierce heat of the sun.

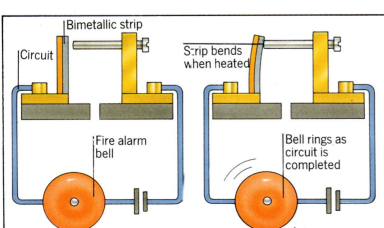

Bimetallic strip

Circuit

Strip bends when heated

Fire alarm bell

Bell rings as circuit is completed

IT RINGS A BELL

This electrical circuit is in a fire alarm system. It consists of a loud bell, an electric circuit, and a bimetallic strip. When the temperature rises beyond a certain level, the strip bends and completes the electric circuit. This causes the bell to ring.

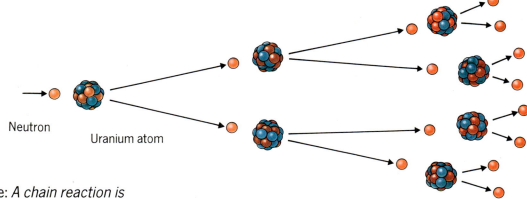

Above: *A chain reaction is an uncontrolled series of nuclear fissions. As the nucleus of a uranium atom is split, the neutrons that emerge split other uranium atoms. The neutrons that emerge from these new fissions split still more atoms, and so on. A tremendous amount of energy is released.*

Below: *The cloud of debris that is thrown into the air by a nuclear explosion.*

Atomic energy – splitting the atom

Nuclear power is the energy released when radioactive atoms are split. Inside a nuclear reactor, this splitting takes place under controlled conditions, producing heat to generate electricity, but in nuclear weapons the energy is released in a violent explosion that causes extensive damage.

Until 1939, it was not thought possible to split an atom, but then, Otto Hahn and Lise Meitner discovered that uranium-235 atoms would divide if they were bombarded with a neutron. (Neutrons are uncharged particles that share the center of atoms with protons.) As a nucleus was split, it produced a large amount of energy and several more neutrons in a process called **fission**. If the newly produced neutrons went on to collide with more nuclei (plural of nucleus), they would make those nuclei split too and release still more neutrons. These neutrons could go on to hit more nuclei and so on, giving an ever-increasing process called a "chain reaction" that actually happens in a fraction of a second. If there is enough uranium, a chain reaction will accelerate uncontrollably—this is what happens in a nuclear bomb.

Inside a nuclear power station

In the "reactor" of a nuclear power station, fission is carefully controlled so that from each atom that splits, only one neutron goes on to split another atom. The extra neutrons are absorbed by the reactor. The fuel used in nuclear reactors is uranium. The fuel is packed into fuel elements that can be fed into the "core" of the reactor. Uranium is a far

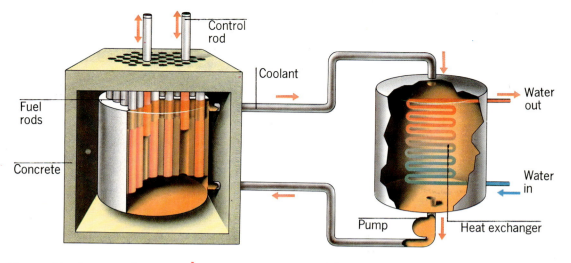

Above: Nuclear reactors, like the one shown here, are enclosed in a thick shield of concrete that prevents the escape of radiation. Within the shield, the heart of the reactor consists of long rods of uranium fuel called elements. Coolant surrounds the elements and absorbs the heat of the reaction. The coolant is then passed through the heat exchanger (on the right) where it transfers the heat to water. The water turns to steam and drives turbines to make electricity.

more concentrated form of energy than coal. A fraction of an ounce of uranium can generate as much electricity as three tons of coal.

To control the surplus neutrons, the fuel is surrounded by a "moderator," a substance that slows down neutrons so that fission keeps going at the correct rate. Fine adjustments to the speed of reaction are made using special "control rods" that can be pushed into the reactor to soak up neutrons and slow it down, or pulled out to speed it up.

The heat produced by the nuclear reactions is absorbed by coolants and used to heat water to drive the turbines. Carbon dioxide gas and water are two substances used as coolants and the newest type of pressurized water reactors (PWRs) use water under high pressure as both a moderator and a coolant. The coolants must flow steadily and constantly past the fuel so that it cannot overheat.

Why does a nuclear reaction produce so much heat?

What happens in a nuclear reaction is quite different from the way in which energy is released from other sources of chemical energy. Burning ten tons of coal releases chemical energy as heat and leaves ten tons of ash plus smoke. But in a nuclear reaction, some of the actual fuel substance is turned into energy, so that there is less total matter left at the end of the reaction.

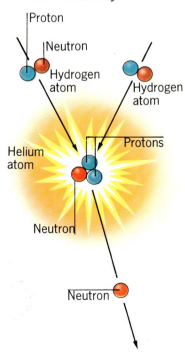

Left: Nuclear energy can be produced in a different process called "fusion." The sun is an enormous nuclear fusion plant. It is so hot that its atoms are moving very fast. Often special hydrogen atoms collide with a force so great that their nuclei fuse together, making a

helium atom. A neutron is released. It is this fusing together of hydrogen atoms to make helium atoms that gives us all the sun's light and heat. On earth, the hydrogen bomb works in a similar way and scientists are trying to tame the power of fusion to provide energy.

Coal – a "fossil" fuel

The sun has shone down on the earth for millions of years, providing energy for plants and animals. Over many centuries, living things have died and their remains have been buried by movements of the earth's crust. Deep down, under great pressure, the remains and their stored energy have formed our "fossil fuels"—peat, coal, oil, and gas.

Coal started to form about 350 million years ago. The remains of swampy forests were compressed and hardened by sand and rocks which were piled on top of them. Gradually the layers of vegetation turned into layers or "seams" of coal, separated by rocks. In some places there are 30 or 40 different seams, one above the other. Together these are called "coal measures."

Coal contains carbon, hydrogen, oxygen, nitrogen, and sulfur molecules. But there are several different types of coal, with different proportions of these elements. Lignite is the youngest type of coal and contains the least carbon. Next comes bituminous coal, which was formed as layers of lignite were squeezed. It takes about 23 feet of vegetation to make a foot of bituminous coal. In a few places, this coal was pressed together with even greater force as mountains were being formed and here a third type of coal—anthracite—has been formed. Anthracite is almost pure carbon and makes hardly any smoke when it burns. But because bituminous coal is cheaper and more plentiful, it is the coal most commonly used to generate electricity in power stations.

Using coal

Coal took over from wood as the main source of fuel for the industrial furnaces of the 18th century. It was used mostly in the growing number of iron smelting works. With the invention of the steam engine, coal became the fuel of the

Coal swamp

Coal

Sandstone

Shale

Coal swamp

Coal

Left: *Fossil fuels come from the remains of plants and animals which lived in the Carboniferous period, 350 million years ago. Seams (layers) of coal formed as coastal swamps containing the remains slowly sank into the sea.*

Industrial Revolution in the 19th century and, by the end of the 1800s, it was being used in the first coal-fired power stations that generated electricity. Today, coal is still used to generate most of the world's electricity.

Coal also has other uses. Much is converted to coke for use in steel-making (see page 75). Coke is made by heating coal inside special coking ovens. Coke is a more compact source of fuel than coal and it contains fewer impurities. In addition, more than 200,000 products, including perfumes, dyes, medicines, and plastics are all made from the coal tar that collects in the chimneys of coking ovens. Until the discovery of natural gas, all the gas supplied to homes was coal gas, produced from the gas given off during the coke-making process. Ammonia, cleaning fluids, fertilizers, and some plastics are just a few of the things that can be made from coal gas, by a process called "carbonization."

Coal itself can be treated to produce gasoline, diesel fuel and kerosene by "hydrogenation." A jet of hydrogen blown through a hot mixture of iron and coal produces a chemical mixture that can be separated into the various fuels.

Above: *Before it can be used, coal must be removed from the ground. Where coal seams are close to the surface, "open cast" mining, shown on the left, is used. In this process, coal is dug at the surface. Underground coal must be reached by digging a "shaft" or "drift" mine. The miners in the photograph on the right are using equipment to remove coal from a seam well below the ground.*

Below Left: *In a deep coal mine, shafts are sunk to reach the coal seams. Miners travel down in a cage. At the coal face, they use cutting machines to remove the coal, which is taken by conveyor belts along tunnels to be loaded onto carts. These carts are then lifted up a shaft to a grading and washing plant on the surface. To keep the air fresh inside the mine, giant fans draw fresh air through the tunnels and suck out stale air. The workings may stretch many miles underground.*

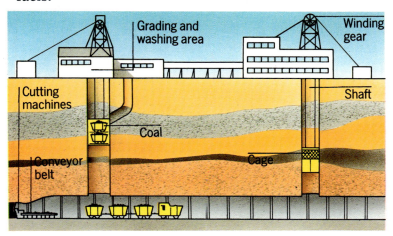

Grading and washing area

Winding gear

Cutting machines

Coal

Shaft

Conveyor belt

Cage

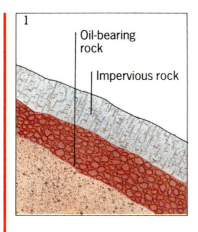

1 Oil-bearing rock
Impervious rock

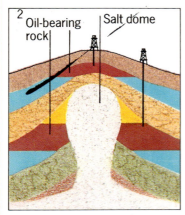

2 Oil-bearing rock Salt dome

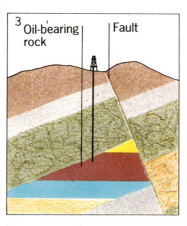

3 Oil-bearing rock Fault

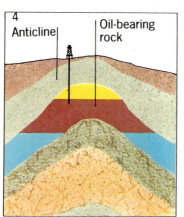

4 Anticline Oil-bearing rock

Oil and natural gas

Oil and gas are also made from the bodies of plants and animals that lived and died millions of years ago. They were formed in conditions of great heat and under great pressure and today they are found only under certain types of rock formation. Depressions in the earth's crust, deep below the surface, often contain oil. It is held in a layer of rock that is full of tiny holes and acts like a sponge. These rocks are trapped between layers of solid rock that do not allow liquid to pass through them. Natural gas is often found lying above a layer of oil-bearing rock, just below the solid layer.

Areas with oil and gas beneath them are not easy to find. Oil has been discovered under the deserts of the Middle East, the swamps of South America, under icefields and under the sea. Geologists survey likely areas using magnetometers and gravitometers which measure the magnetism and hardness of the rock formations below. A seismograph survey, to show how various layers are arranged, is carried out by setting off a small explosion on the surface and recording the shock waves that are bounced back from the earth's crust beneath.

Oil is reached by drilling a well. A drilling rig on land has a huge tower called a "derrick" to house the equipment. On an offshore rig, the derrick is often carried on an enormous floating platform. A derrick is rather like an upright crane. Pipes for carrying the oil up to the surface can be winched up and down to the drill, which bores down into the ground. As the drill goes deeper and deeper, additional lengths of pipe are attached behind it and the sides of the wall are lined with steel to stop it caving in. Water and chemicals are pumped down the well to clear away fragments of rock and lubricate the bit (the cutting end of the drill).

Once oil has been found, the derrick is no longer needed. On land, all that is left on the top of the well is a "christmas tree"—a set of valves which can be opened to

Oil is held as drops between grains of oil-bearing rock (1). It seeps up through porous (permeable) rock, such as sandstone, until it is stopped by impervious rock, such as granite. Layers of oil can be trapped in various ways. (2) Salt domes can keep oil from flowing to the surface. (3) Oil can be trapped by a "fault" (movement) in the earth's crust. Here, a layer of rock has slipped and trapped some oil. (4) Some layers of rock are arranged in an arch called an "anticline." If the top layers are impervious rock, the oil cannot seep upward and is trapped below in a pool.

Left: *An oil production platform. Much of our oil comes from under the sea.*
Below left: *The laying of oil and natural gas pipelines is often difficult. Here a gas pipe has to cross a river.*
Bottom left: *A diamond-tipped bit is used for drilling through very hard rock. It can be worn out after just a few hundred yards.*
Bottom center: *Drilling for oil is tiring and dirty work. The man shown here is inspecting a different type of bit—one used to drill through soft rock.*
Below: *A diagram of a drilling rig. The hole drilled at the top of an oil well can be 5 feet across, but far below the surface it will be only 6 inches.*

allow oil, or oil and gas, to flow out when they are needed. At sea, a production platform is set up to store oil in its tanks and pump it ashore. Pipelines carry oil and gas across land or under water to terminals, where the two are separated. From the terminal, oil goes on to the refinery, while gas can be pumped to homes and factories.

Natural gas consists mainly of methane, which has no smell. Strong-smelling chemicals are added to the gas for safety reasons so that any gas leakage can be detected. Natural gas is not only used for heating and cooking, some is used to manufacture other chemicals such as alcohol and butane and it is also a source of helium gas.

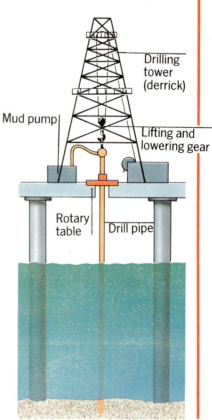

Drilling tower (derrick)

Mud pump

Lifting and lowering gear

Rotary table

Drill pipe

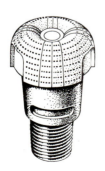

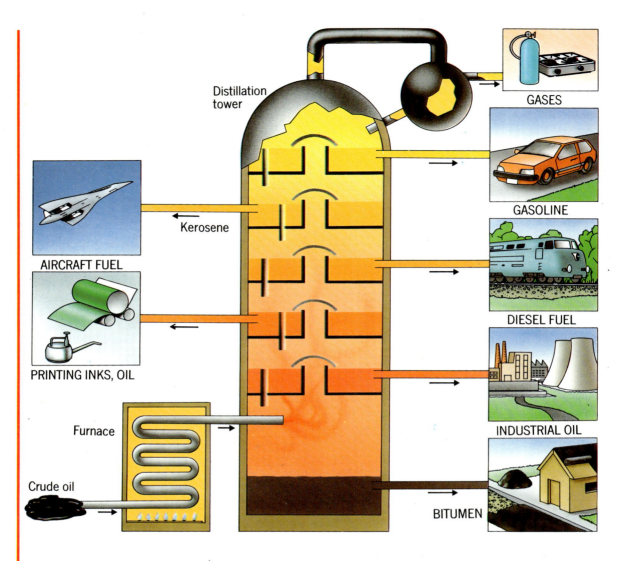

Distillation tower

GASES

Kerosene

GASOLINE

AIRCRAFT FUEL

DIESEL FUEL

PRINTING INKS, OIL

INDUSTRIAL OIL

Furnace

Crude oil

BITUMEN

Preparing oil for use

The "crude" (unrefined) oil which comes out of the ground is a mixture of many substances. Before it can be used as a fuel or in the manufacture of other products, it must be processed in a refinery. The first stage in refining oil is **distillation**. Crude oil is heated to 750°F in a furnace. When it boils, the oil turns to a mixture of gases and vapors which rise up inside tall towers called "distillation columns." As they travel up the columns, different parts —"fractions"—of the vapors cool and turn back into liquid at different heights. As they do this, they are collected as a variety of products in special distillation trays. The heaviest liquids, such as heavy fuel oils, form and are drawn off at the bottom of the column, the lightest, such as gasoline, come out at the top. The residue left at the end of the process is called bitumen. Bitumen is used for surfacing roads or it can be refined again to make lubricating oils and waxes.

Another process, called "catalytic cracking," can be used to break down heavy oils from the column into lighter

Above: *Crude oil is broken down into its various "fractions" (parts) by "fractional distillation." The crude oil is heated to a vapor at the bottom of a tall tower. As the vapor passes up the tower, different products are drawn off. Toward the top of the column come kerosene for aircraft fuel, diesel oil and gasoline. Right at the top, fuel gas comes off. Heavy products, such as asphalt for road-making and heavy fuel oils, sink to the bottom. Some products, such as gasoline and kerosene, are refined further.*

ones. Cracking means breaking up large molecules into smaller ones. It is used to make gasoline. Inside a "cat cracker" heavy oil and steam are passed up a column. The trays inside this column are filled with a catalyst (a chemical substance that makes a reaction happen but does not react itself). By using different catalysts, different proportions of the various products can be collected. Catalytic cracking can produce twice as much gasoline as ordinary refining.

Oil provides fuel for industrial blast furnaces and for about 20 percent of the world's power stations. But burning oil is not a very efficient way of producing electricity. Only about 35 percent of the energy in the oil is converted into electricity. But oil continues to be used because oil-fired power stations are cheap to build and maintain. Countless products all around us are made from the chemicals that are derived from oil, including detergents, plastics, cosmetics, drugs, fertilizers, and animal foods.

Because oil from wells is gradually running out, new sources are being investigated. Canada has thick beds of bitumen-coated gravel from which oil can be extracted. The Orinoco oil belt of Venezuela is an area that is full of tar and pitch, and oil-rich rocks called "shale" have been found in Brazil and the U.S.S.R. Until recently these sources of oil were too costly to exploit, but as oil becomes scarcer and more expensive, they could provide a vital new supply.

For the same reasons, more attention is being given to the way these fuels are used. The long-term importance of fuel economy is understood the world over.

Below: *Thousands of products are made from the chemicals that come from oil. Plastics—from shirts and stockings to rope and records—are oil-based. So are an assortment of things such as paint, tires, detergents, cosmetics, animal feed, and fertilizers.*

Vinyl

Household detergents/ cleaners

Nylon

Synthetic rubber

Polyester

Polyethylene

Cosmetics

Polyurethane

Vinyl

Soap

Nylon

Animal feed

10. Putting Science to Work

Plastics

We are surrounded by plastics—hundreds of different types. Some are as strong as steel. Others are as soft as wool. Some will resist a fierce flame. Others will melt in hot water. But they have all been made by chemists.

The first plastic was celluloid. It was tough, but it burned fiercely. Now it is only used to make tabletennis balls. Then, in 1907, came Bakelite (see page 107), a substance that could be used for anything from light fittings to billiard balls.

Below: *Stages in the production of nylon fiber. A chemical called caprolactam is heated under pressure to make long polymer filaments which are melted and pumped through tiny holes. The threads harden in the air; then they are twisted together to make nylon yarn.*

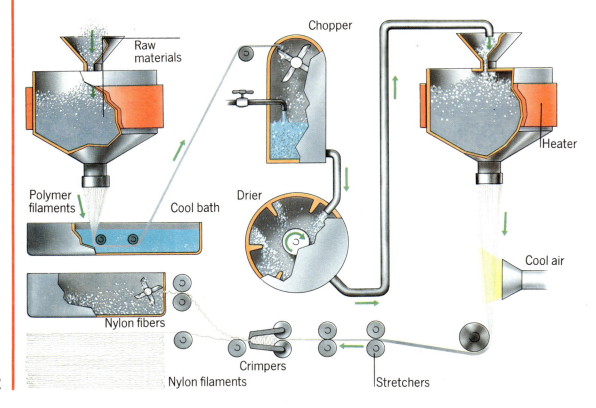

Raw materials

Chopper

Heater

Polymer filaments

Cool bath

Drier

Cool air

Nylon fibers

Crimpers

Nylon filaments

Stretchers

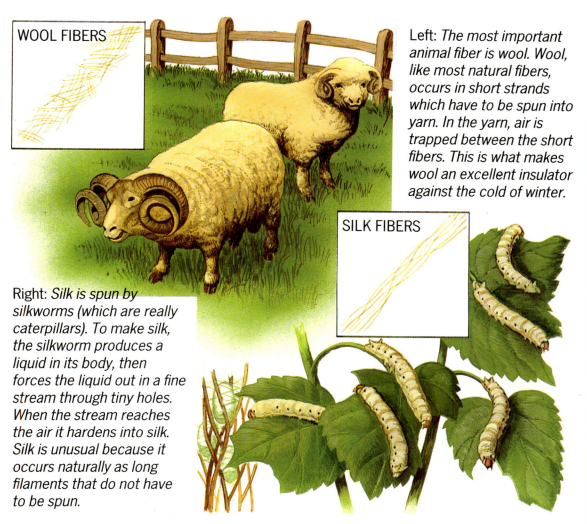

WOOL FIBERS

SILK FIBERS

Left: *The most important animal fiber is wool. Wool, like most natural fibers, occurs in short strands which have to be spun into yarn. In the yarn, air is trapped between the short fibers. This is what makes wool an excellent insulator against the cold of winter.*

Right: *Silk is spun by silkworms (which are really caterpillars). To make silk, the silkworm produces a liquid in its body, then forces the liquid out in a fine stream through tiny holes. When the stream reaches the air it hardens into silk. Silk is unusual because it occurs naturally as long filaments that do not have to be spun.*

What are plastics?

All plastics belong to a family of chemicals called "polymers"—materials that have long chain-like molecules made up of hundreds of similar units linked together. There are two main kinds of plastic—"thermosetting plastics" and "thermoplastics." Thermosetting plastics do not melt when they are heated. They get even harder. Thermoplastics can be melted and hardened again time after time. The main thermoplastics are polyethylene (polythene), first made in large quantities in 1953, PVC, and polystyrene.

Hot, soft plastic can be shaped in different ways. In "injection molding," a thermoplastic is made liquid by heating and then being squirted under pressure into a closed mold. When it is cooled it becomes solid and is pushed out when the mold is opened. Hollow shapes such as bottles are usually formed by "blow molding." The soft plastic is forced against the walls of the mold by air pressure inside. Plastics are also processed by "extrusion." Here the soft material is squeezed through holes or slits to form plastic rods, tubes or sheets. "Calendering" is putting a thin coat of heat-softened plastic on cloth. The

Above: *Natural fibers are threads obtained from animals and plants. Fibers can be twisted together to make strong, useful materials. Sheep's wool is the best known animal fiber, but there are many others. Goats, llamas, alpacas, rabbits, and camels all give us fibers that can be made into cloth. Silk is the only important fiber that we get from an insect. Most fibers are short, ranging in length from only half an inch to 4 inches long. Before they can be woven into fabrics they have to be spun or twisted together to form yarns.*

103

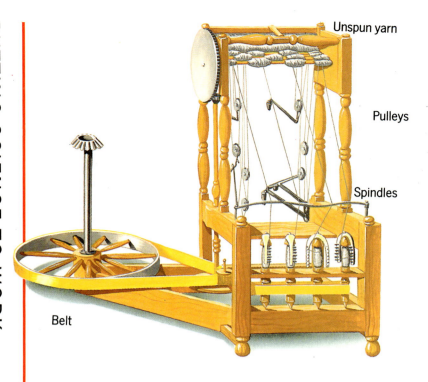

Unspun yarn

Pulleys

Spindles

Belt

Left: *When Richard Arkwright (1732–92) invented the "Spinning Jenny" he revolutionized the textile industry. This spinning machine produced thread on several spindles at once and was driven by an engine. It was much faster than making yarn by hand. Unspun yarn was pulled and twisted through rollers at the top. Threads were kept tight by pulleys and were wound around the spindles below. The machine was driven by a steam engine that turned a belt. The belt was connected to the machine by a series of gears.*

plastic-coated cloth is put under pressure by running it through heated, metal rollers. This presses the plastic into the fibers of the cloth. Certain kinds of rainwear, tents, and tablecloths are made by calendering.

In "laminating," a sandwich is made by placing layers of plastic powder between layers of glass or wood. The sandwich is put under heat and pressure. The plastic powder melts and seals the layers of glass or wood together, forming a strong sheet. Safety glass for car windshields and plywood are made by lamination.

Nearly all modern plastics are made from light gases

Below: *Cloth is made by weaving threads together on a loom. Rows of threads called warp threads are attached to the loom and stretched lengthwise through holes in wires called "healds." The healds are attached to a frame called a "heddle." During weaving, the healds raise and lower alternate threads. This creates a gap through which the weft thread is carried to and fro by the shuttle. To get patterns, combinations of warp threads can be moved.*

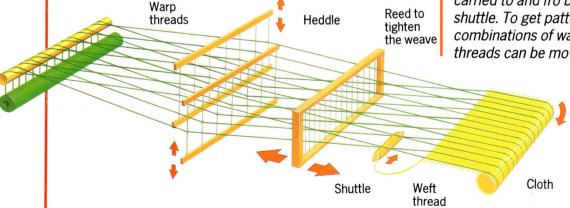

Warp threads

Heddle

Reed to tighten the weave

Shuttle

Weft thread

Cloth

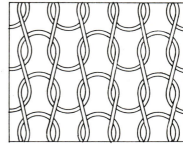

Left: *Modern wide machines allow manufacturers to print fabrics at high speed.*

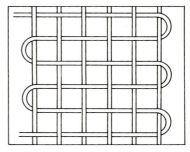

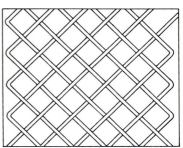

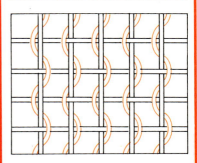

Making clothes

The materials that we use to make our clothes are made from threads or fibers which are woven into cloth. Some are "natural" fibers from animals, plants, or even minerals, while "man-made" fibers are manufactured.

The two most common types of plant fibers are cotton and flax. Cotton fibers come from inside the seed pod or "boll" of cotton plants. Flax plants produce the fibers that are used to make linen cloth. The lower parts of the stem and the roots of the plants provide the best fibers.

Wool and silk are the best-known animal fibers. Wool comes from the soft hair—the fleece—of a sheep. But other animals also provide wool for clothing. For example, goats provide mohair and rabbits provide angora. Silk comes from the cocoons of the silkworm. The caterpillars of the silk moth spin more than 3,000 feet of silk around themselves in about three days. This silk thread can then be unwound and used to make soft fabric that is both shiny and strong.

Man-made fibers are sold under many brand names such as Terylene (polyester) and Courtelle (acrylic). All man-made fibers are slightly different but they can be divided into two main types: **cellulose** fibers, which are made from cellulose extracted from natural fibers of trees and plants, and **synthetic** fibers, which are made from coal and oil products (see page 100). The cellulose fibers used to make rayon, acetate, and triacetate fabric come

Above: *Different patterns in cloth are made by different kinds of weaving. From the top: Looped weft threads; weft threads woven in and out of warp threads; plaited weave; third thread added to a plain (criss-cross) weave. Most cloth is plain weave.*

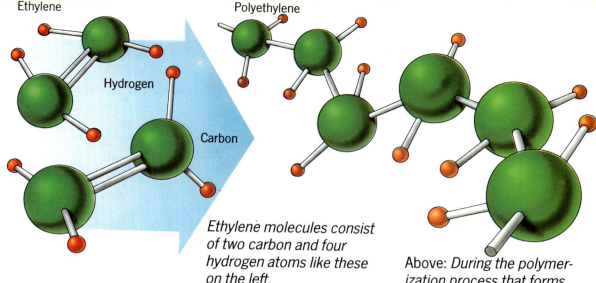

Ethylene

Polyethylene

Hydrogen

Carbon

Ethylene molecules consist of two carbon and four hydrogen atoms like these on the left.

Above: *During the polymerization process that forms polyethylene, the ethylene molecules form long chains. Many plastics begin with poly ("many") because they are chains of units.*

Below: *How polyethylene (polythene) is made. Ethylene molecules are made into long chains by being heated and compressed. The plastic is then formed into sheets.*

from the wood of spruce trees and from cotton linters (short cotton fibers). Synthetic fibers, such as polyester and acrylic, are made by polymerization (see page 102).

Spinning and weaving

All natural fibers reach the spinning mill in a "raw" condition, complete with dirt, leaves and tangles. So the first step in the spinning process is cleaning. Raw cotton is broken up and knocked back and forth to loosen dirt and separate lumps before being cleaned, while wool is washed to remove grease and dirt. Flax for linen cloth is "hackled"—a process which removes woody particles and combs the flax fibers straight.

Making yarn

The fibers of all three products then move on to the "carding" machine. Here they are untangled and combed. Short fibers weaken the yarn which is to be produced, so these are removed. At the end of the carding process, the fibers come out as a rope of straight fibers called a "sliver." Several slivers are stretched together through rollers and slightly twisted, ready to be spun into continuous lengths of "yarn" that, in turn, can be woven into cloth.

All natural fibers and man-made cellulose fibers are spun by drawing (or pulling), twisting and winding into fine,

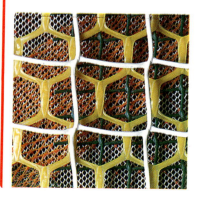

Left: *All these nets are made from molded or woven plastics. The strong white net is used in soccer goals, the fine orange net may hold oranges in a supermarket, while the yellow and green nets could be used to cover garden plants.*

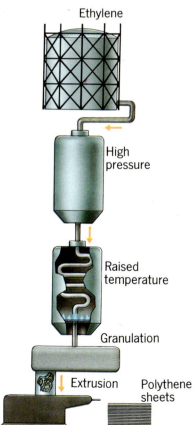

Ethylene

High pressure

Raised temperature

Granulation

Extrusion

Polythene sheets

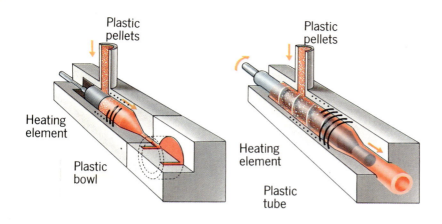

Plastic pellets

Heating element

Plastic bowl

Plastic pellets

Heating element

Plastic tube

On the left, hot plastic is being squeezed—extruded—into a long thin tube shape by forcing it through a specially shaped hole. On the far left, a bowl is being made by "injection molding." Hot plastic is forced into a mold which is cooled to harden the plastic.

strong threads. Often, different fibers are spun together to produce combinations such as cotton-polyester, which has the softness of cotton plus the crease-resistance of polyester. Silk and synthetic man-made fibers do not need to be spun because they are already in long continuous lengths. However, several strands of silk are usually twisted together to give a stronger yarn.

Making material
Weaving is a process that intertwines the threads of yarn to form a fabric. Threads are built up into patterns under and over one another on a machine called a loom. The threads of the cloth that run lengthwise are fixed to the loom and are called **warp** threads. **Weft** threads are woven under and over the warp threads. Usually the weft threads are carried to and fro across the warp threads by a shuttle, although modern shuttleless looms use a jet of air or water to carry them.

Not all fabrics are made by weaving. Knitting is a different process that entwines loops of yarn in rows. Commercial knitting machines use hundreds of needles to produce either tubes or lengths of knitted fabric. Felt is another fabric that is not woven. It is made by compressing layers of wet wool fibers together. Felt is one of the oldest fabrics and has been made for hundreds of years.

THE FIRST PLASTIC
Bakelite was invented in 1908 by Henry Baekland. As it was a good insulator, it was ideal for electrical equipment. Early phonograph records were made of bakelite and it was popular until the 1950s.

Platform

Foot-operated treadle

Wheel

Left: *The potter's wheel has a platform at the top. It is here that the potter shapes the clay. The platform turns as the potter operates the wheel at the bottom with his or her feet.*

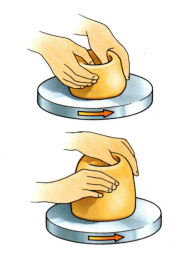

All kinds of pottery

All the china and pottery objects that we use are made from clay—a mineral consisting mostly of aluminum silicate dug from clay pits in the ground. Mixed with water, clay is soft and flexible and can be formed into shapes. But when clay is heated, it dries out and binds together and can never be softened again.

Thousands of years ago, people used clay to make brown earthenware pots that were dried in the sun. Later, about 1,500 years ago, the Chinese made the first porcelain, a thin, strong, white pottery made with special, fine white clay. We call this clay "china clay" and this is why the name "china" is used to describe delicate types of pottery. In 1794 another type of china, called "bone china" was made in England by Josiah Spode. This was made by mixing crushed, burned animal bones with china clay and the mineral feldspar (or "china stone").

Whatever the type of pottery that is being made, the first stage in the process is always to mix the clay with water. This liquid clay is called "slip." Slip can be used to fill plaster molds to produce hollow pots such as jugs and coffee pots. To make vases, cups, and plates, water can be pressed out of the slip to leave a firmer clay called "body

Above: *Shaping a pot on a wheel is known as "turning." The potter holds a lump of clay on the rotating platform until it is a round shape. Next, the thumbs are pressed into the center of the clay so that the inside is hollowed out. Finally, the hands are eased upward to make a tall shape.*

Below: *In a china factory, a hollow pot can be made by pouring "slip"—molten clay— into a mold. Water seeps out of the slip into the mold and so the clay next to the mold begins to harden. When the required thickness of clay has hardened, the remaining slip can be poured away to leave a hollow shape.*

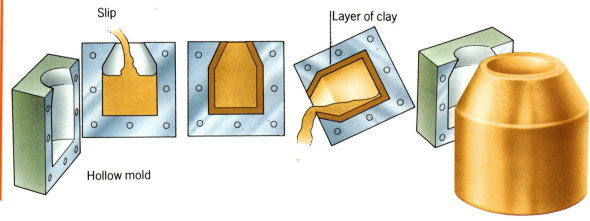

Slip

Layer of clay

Hollow mold

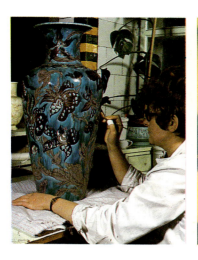

Left: *Another word for pottery is "ceramics." This is a broad term used to mean materials from the earth that are baked. Here are two very different examples. On the far left is a huge urn made of porcelain—a fine pottery—being delicately hand painted.*

Next to this is an unusual ceramic—part of a tile used on the space shuttle. It is made of silica fibers. These fibers form a "refractory" material. A refractory material is one that is very heat resistant, in fact these tiles are one of the best insulators known.

clay." Body clay can be formed to the required shapes on a potter's wheel or in molds as shown in the diagrams on the left.

Clay shapes are hardened by "firing" (baking) them in a kiln. Early potters used dome-shaped kilns heated by wood, but modern potteries use long "tunnel kilns" heated by gas or electricity. Trolley-loads of pots move along the tunnels, which are cool at both ends but very hot in the center. The pots must be heated in the kiln for about 60 hours to harden them completely.

Most pottery is decorated and given a shiny finish called a "glaze." Glaze makes the hardened clay resistant to water which would otherwise soak into it. Objects can either be dipped into the glaze or it can be sprayed on. To set the glaze, the pottery has to be fired for a second time in the kiln.

Pottery makes a good insulator because it does not conduct electricity. It is used not only for cups, saucers, and plates, but also for parts of lamps, high-voltage electrical connectors, and even for sections of car spark plugs. Different types of clay are also used to make bricks and roof tiles for our homes.

Below: *This box shows how cement is made. Cement is another "ceramic" (see caption above) material. It is the vital ingredient of concrete and, like clay, can only be shaped when wet.*

Cement is mainly a mixture of limestone and clay, with other ingredients added, depending on the type of concrete wanted.

HOW CEMENT IS MADE

Water is added to a mixture of crushed limestone and clay. The slurry is then burned in giant kilns and ground to a fine powder.

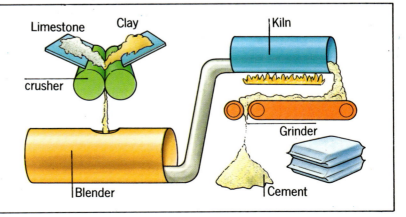

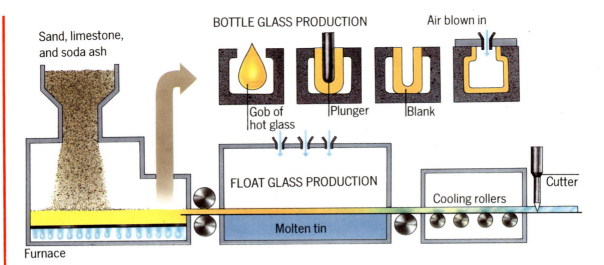

Sand, limestone, and soda ash

BOTTLE GLASS PRODUCTION

Air blown in

Gob of hot glass

Plunger

Blank

FLOAT GLASS PRODUCTION

Cooling rollers

Cutter

Molten tin

Furnace

Glass

Glass is one of the oldest man-made materials. The first glass was probably made in Egypt in about 3000 B.C. by people who used colored glazes on their pottery. Today, glass is still an essential part of life. It has the advantage of being easily shaped, rust-proof and hygienic, and can be recycled to be used over and over again.

The main ingredients of glass are silica (which comes from sand), soda ash, and limestone. To make special types of glass, such as lead crystal glass or heat-resistant glass, other chemicals may be added as well. These ingredients, to which coloring agents may also be added, are heated until they melt. Until this century, most glass was made by "blowing" (see photograph below).

Today, some glass, particularly delicate ornamental glass, is still made by hand. However, most of it is

Above: *Glass manufacture. Silica, soda ash, and limestone are loaded into the furnace, along with "cullet"—old bits of glass. Molten glass from the furnace may either be molded and blown into hollow shapes (above), or shaped into flat sheets by the "float glass" method (below). In the float glass process, molten glass is floated on a "bath" of molten tin and then cooled and cut into lengths.*

Right: *Here, float glass is having its edges automatically trimmed as it moves over rollers.*
Inset: *The traditional way of making glass objects. "Gobs" of molten glass are placed on the end of a long tube. Blowing down the tube produces a bubble that can be shaped before it cools. Once, even window glass was made like this— the huge bubble could be flattened and "turned" (twirled and trimmed) to give a piece of flat glass.*

110

Left: *Glass can be used for countless things, but perhaps one of its most dramatic uses is in stained glass church windows. This beautiful window is in Liverpool Cathedral, England.*

produced by machines. The mixed ingredients are melted in huge furnaces at a temperature of 2,700°F. This gives a flow of liquid glass that can be shaped by special forming machines. Vast amounts of clear sheet glass are made by the "float glass" method—invented by Sir Alastair Pilkington in 1959. The ribbon of molten glass flows into a tank called a float bath. This bath is filled with molten tin and the hot glass floats on the smooth, flat surface of the tin. As the glass moves through the bath, the temperature is lowered so that the glass begins to harden. Then, the sheets can be moved over rollers to be cooled slowly.

Glass for bottles and jars is also made in a mechanized process. Molten glass made in a furnace is pushed through an "orifice ring"—a sort of bowl with a hole in it—then cut into pieces called "gobs." The gobs are usually pressed into shape in molds, if they are to become jars, dishes, or bowls. If they are to become bottles, or containers with narrow necks, the gobs will probably be blown up automatically inside molds by jets of compressed air. Whatever shape the formed glass takes, it must be cooled slowly so that it shrinks evenly and doesn't crack.

Versatile glass

As well as bottles and jars, glass also has some very specialized uses. One is in lenses for eyeglasses and cameras. This type is called optical glass and must be completely free of any faults or bubbles. When it has been melted in the furnace, optical glass is cast into blocks or shaped into bars. These can then be remolded, ground and polished to the correct shapes and sizes. "Fiber glass" consists of plastic strengthened with fibers (threads) of glass. Because it is both light and strong, it is ideal for making boat hulls and car bodies. One of the newest uses for glass is in optical fibers for telecommunications (see page 40). To make them, glass rods are heated with care and stretched into fine, high-quality strands.

Below: *Glass can be drawn out into long threads by pouring red-hot molten glass through the bottom of a furnace.*

This thread has many uses, such as in sound and heat insulation in buildings and around boilers and in fire resistant clothes. One important use is in "fiber glass." For this, it is combined with plastic to give an easily molded, light and strong substance ideal for making boat hulls and car bodies.

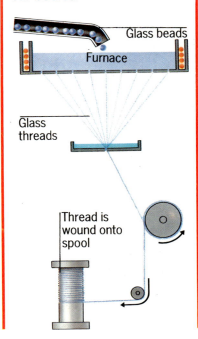

Glass beads

Furnace

Glass threads

Thread is wound onto spool

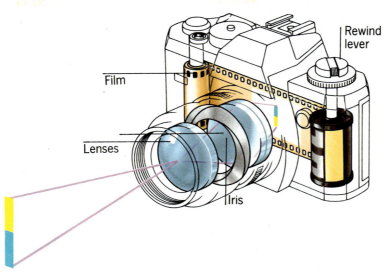

Film

Lenses

Iris

Rewind lever

Photography— painting with light

Before photography, the only way to record people and places was by sketching or painting. Louis Daguerre and Joseph Niepce produced the first photograph in 1826, on a copper plate treated with light-sensitive chemicals. Plates like this became known as "daguerreotypes." But, in 1835, Fox Talbot produced prints from small negatives and by 1888, George Eastman had made the first modern camera—the Kodak—and the first rolls of film.

Early cameras were simply boxes that let no light in, with light-sensitive paper at the back and a lens at the front. Instead of an automatic shutter letting in a certain amount of light, a lens cap had to be removed by hand, for up to several minutes. The subjects had to keep very still all this time so that the final image was not blurred!

Cameras today still work on the same principles. As you press the shutter-release, you allow light through the lens onto the film at the back. The image made on the film is "negative"—the dark areas of the subject appear light and the light areas dark—but when the film has been processed, the image is seen correctly. To adjust the amount of light that falls on the film, the lens may have an aperture (opening) that can be made larger or smaller—in dim conditions it can be opened further to let in more light or opened less in bright conditions.

Photography is possible because light makes certain silver compounds—in particular silver bromide—turn black when treated with the appropriate chemicals. Film is made of plastic, with at least one layer of a light-sensitive emulsion on one side. Black and white film has one layer, while color film has three—one sensitive to red, one to blue, and one to yellow. Light from the subject being

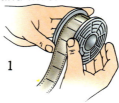

1

1. The film is wound around a special holder. This is done in a dark room.

Developer

Stop bath

Fixer

2

2. The holder is fixed inside a tank. Developer, stop bath, and fixer are added in turn, for precise periods of time.

Water

3

3. A water hose is attached to the tank and the film is carefully washed.

4

4. Finally the film is removed with tongs and hung up to dry.

The flash unit on a camera is designed to give a brief flare of intense artificial light—enough to take a photograph where there is too little natural light. Most cameras with built-in flash produce this flare electronically, as a sudden burst of electricity passes between two electrodes inside a glass chamber. Below: Printing black and white film.

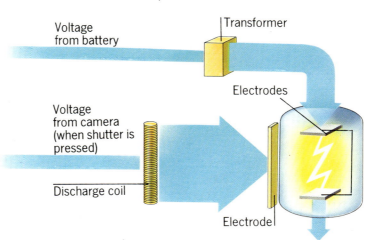

Voltage from battery

Transformer

Electrodes

Voltage from camera (when shutter is pressed)

Discharge coil

Electrode

1. The negative is placed in a holder below the lens of an enlarger.

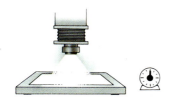

2. Light is shone through the negative onto photographic paper below.

3. The print is processed in trays of developer, stop bath, and fixer.

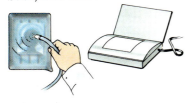

4. The print is washed then dried on an electrically heated metal "flat bed."

photographed strikes the emulsion and changes it to silver. The stronger the light, the greater the reaction. As the film is processed, the parts that were exposed to light are completely changed to silver, and those that were not exposed have the unchanged silver bromide removed from them. When color films are processed, the exposed parts of the film are replaced with colored dyes.

The first stage of processing film is to place it in "developer"—a chemical that turns light-activated silver to gray or black silver. The shade depends on the amount of light that struck the film. This process gives a negative image. Next, the film is washed and then soaked in "fixer"—a chemical that dissolves away any remaining silver bromide and stops film from being further affected by light.

With developing and fixing complete, prints can be made from the negatives, usually with the help of a piece of equipment called an "enlarger." A negative is placed on a platform above a convex lens and a sheet of light-sensitive paper is placed below the lens. A strong light is shone briefly down through the negative. The negative image is enlarged as it passes through the convex lens, onto the paper below. This paper also has a layer of light-sensitive emulsion, the same as film. Black and white paper has one layer of emulsion and color has three, just like film. Darker areas of the negative let through less light onto the paper and light areas let through more—so the print image reverses the negative one. The print is developed and fixed in the same way as film is.

Flash units let us take photographs when natural light is dim, but we can also take photographs in the dark, by using infrared sensitive film. An infrared photograph shows the pattern of heat given out by a subject. It can be used at night to take photographs through clouds and fog. The long wavelength of infrared rays means that they are not scattered off course by the water droplets that make up clouds, as visible light waves are.

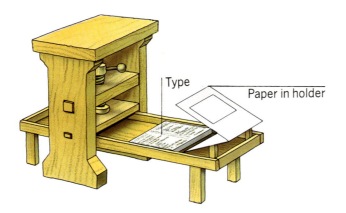

Type

Paper in holder

Printing—spreading the word

Printing in its most simple form was invented in China more than 1,000 years ago. A flat wooden block was carved to form a raised letter or design and covered with ink. A piece of paper pressed down on the block became printed with the block's design.

In the 15th century, Johannes Gutenberg invented the first mechanical printing press. He also devised a method of making individual letters from small pieces of metal. Each letter—"type"—was a raised surface on a metal block and could be arranged—"set"—by hand to form words and sentences. This movable type could be used over and over again after printing had been completed. This basic principle is called "letterpress" printing.

Today, type is no longer set by hand—typesetting machines are used instead. Someone types the "copy" (the words to be printed) into a keyboard like that on a typewriter. Letters are automatically produced in the form of metal or, more commonly, film.

But sentences have to be made up into whole pages, ready to be printed. (Some systems allow you to design and assemble each page by typing instructions into a computer that shows you the page layout on a small screen.) Pages are printed from metal plates. Some have the page's contents as a raised surface pattern in the

Below: "Phototypesetting"— how most type is now prepared for printing. Words and instructions are typed into a keyboard and processed by a computer. This passes to a machine that produces the words, photographically, on film or paper. This can now be used to produce plates, ready for printing.

Keyboard

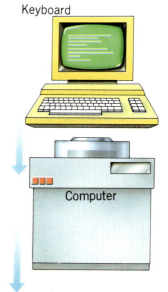

Computer

Left: Gutenberg's first printing press was made from an adapted wine press. All early presses were made of wood. To press the paper down onto the type, a huge screw had to be turned to force a heavy wooden board down onto the paper.

Phototypesetter

metal. But usually, the plate has a light-sensitive covering that reacts by hardening when a photographic image of the page is shone onto it. Areas that are unaffected wash away, while the hard areas are left as a raised image that takes ink. But a huge amount of modern printing is done with totally flat plates. This is called "photolithography" and the plates are also prepared photographically.

Once plates have been prepared, printing can begin. There are two main types of printing press—"rotary" and "offset lithography." Some hold the plates vertically, while others bend the plates around large cylinders. "Sheet-fed" presses have paper fed in to be printed one sheet at a time, while "web-fed" presses use continuous rolls of paper that are cut into pages after printing.

The commonest type of printing press is the offset lithography press. This uses a system of cylinders and rollers and ink is transferred—offset—from the plate onto a rubber blanket and from the blanket to the paper.

Color images have to be "separated"—broken down into yellow, magenta (pinky red), cyan (blue), and black images. These are then printed one on top of the other to produce the final, full-color version. So there are plates for each of these colors for every page of a book or magazine that has color pictures and text in. This is where the term "four color printing" comes from (three colors plus black).

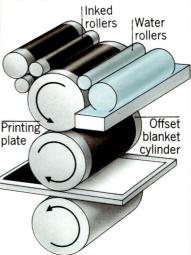

Inked rollers | Water rollers

Printing plate

Offset blanket cylinder

Above: *An offset lithography printing press uses a system of inked rollers to transfer ink to the large cylinder that holds the printing plate. Then ink is transferred or "offset" from the plate to a rubber blanket and onto the paper.*

A printing plate is made for each color and each color is printed on top of the other, to produce the final image.

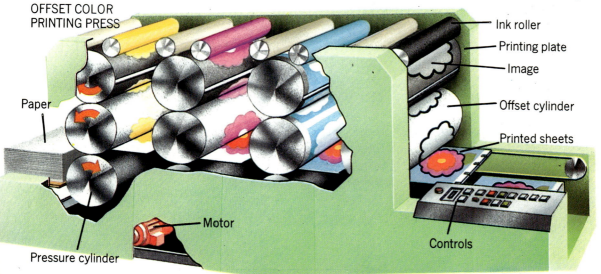

OFFSET COLOR PRINTING PRESS

Paper

Motor

Pressure cylinder

Ink roller

Printing plate

Image

Offset cylinder

Printed sheets

Controls

11. Backward and Forward

Discoveries and inventions

Above: *A model of an early reflecting telescope, from the 1600s.*

Below: *Alexander Graham Bell's telephone. His first message was to a Mr. Watson, on another floor of the building. Bell was asking Watson to come and help him as he had just spilled some acid over himself!*

1450s Johannes Gutenberg invented movable type.

1590 Zacharias Janssen built the first microscope.

1608 Hans Lippershey made the first telescope.

1672 Otto von Guericke made the first electrical device —a ball of sulfur charged with static electricity.

1733 John Kay invented the "flying shuttle," which speeded up the process of weaving.

1766 Hydrogen discovered by Henry Cavendish.

1772 Nitrogen discovered by Daniel Rutherford.

1774 Oxygen discovered by Joseph Priestley and Karl Scheele.

1800 Alessandro Volta built the "voltaic pile"—the forerunner of the battery.

1807 John Dalton proposed his atomic theory to explain the structure of matter.

1820s Electromagnetism was discovered by Hans Oersted and the theory of the electric motor was proposed by Michael Faraday. William Sturgeon built the first working electric motor and later, the first useful electromagnet.

1826 Niepce made a photographic image on a copper plate coated with bitumen and André Ampère put forward his laws of electric conduction and magnetism.

1827 Georg Ohm published laws governing electric conduction and resistance.

1831 Michael Faraday made the first generator.

1864 James Clerk Maxwell outlined the theory of light waves as part of the electromagnetic spectrum.

1876 Alexander Graham Bell passed a voice along a wire—he had invented the telephone. Nicholas Otto built the first internal-combustion engine.

1877	Thomas Edison built a "phonograph" that could record a human voice.
1880s	Count Hilaire de Chardonnet made rayon—the first man-made fiber.
1887	Heinrich Hertz discovered radio waves.
1889	Thomas Edison made a "kinetograph" to take moving pictures and a "kinetoscope" to show them.
1895	Wilhelm Roentgen discovered X-rays.
1896	Antoine Becquerel detected rays coming from a piece of uranium. These were later said to be radiation by Marie Curie.
1898	Radium was discovered by Marie and Pierre Curie.
1901	Guglielmo Marconi sent the first radio signals across the Atlantic.
1904	The thermionic tube was invented by John Ambrose Fleming.
1905	Albert Einstein proposed his Theory of Relativity and predicted the future possibility of nuclear power.
1911	Ernest Rutherford and Niels Bohr made the first model of the structure of an atom.
1926	John Logie Baird built the first primitive television.
1942	Enrico Fermi and a team of physicists built the first nuclear reactor in Chicago.
1944	The first digital computer was built by Howard Aitken at Harvard University.
1947	Bardeen, Shockley, and Brattain built the first transistors while working for the Bell Telephone Company.
1949	Denis Gabor proposed a way of making three-dimensional photographs by holography.
1956	Videotape recording was pioneered by A. Poniatoff.
1958	Nobel prize awarded to Townes, Basoc, and Prokhorov for discovering the laser.
1960	Charles Maiman built the first ruby laser.
1961	The first silicon chip was patented in Dallas, Texas.
1969	*Apollo II* astronauts Neil Armstrong and Buzz (Edwin) Aldrin landed on the moon.
1973	Godfrey Hounsfield developed a "body scanner" that takes detailed X-ray pictures of fine "slices" of the inside of the body. The first computer-controlled laser was used—to cut cloth in the manufacture of men's clothes.
1987	Nobel prize for physics is awarded to Drs. Müller and Bednorz for their research into super-conductivity (see over page).

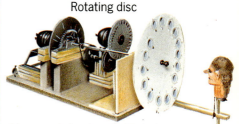

Rotating disc

Above: *John Logie Baird demonstrated the first TV in 1925. Light from the doll's head filtered through holes in a rotating disc. This was turned into electrical signals and back into a beam of light that was projected onto a screen.*

Above: *"reel to reel" tape recorders, common in the 1960s, were much more bulky and fiddly to use than modern cassettes.*

Below: *A body scanner takes X-ray pictures from many different angles and then produces a full, computerized picture.*

Looking to the future

Physicists and engineers have transformed travel during this century with the invention of the internal-combustion engine (1876), the jet engine (1930), and the air cushion vehicle (1959). Gasoline-powered vehicles are convenient, but they cause pollution and use our diminishing oil supplies. The latest solar powered cars do not have these drawbacks and, with their streamlined shapes, can travel almost as fast as the cars we use at the moment.

Medicine also continues to develop through new technology. X-rays, discovered in 1895, gave doctors their first method of looking inside the body. Now, doctors have the ability to "scan" the inside of patients' bodies in much more detail and process the information with computers. They can use X-rays (page 117), sound waves (page 29), radio waves, and radioactive substances.

Above: *The car on the right is powered by solar energy, captured by the solar panels on the top. It is able to travel almost as fast as gasoline-driven cars and raced across Australia in a Solar Challenge Race. One day cars like it may send all gasoline-driven vehicles to the scrap heap!*

Left: *Soon, more and more people will buy their own dish antennas, perhaps from a "drive-in" store like this one in Nevada. Mounted on the roof or in the garden, these dishes pick up signals sent to space satellites by television stations thousands of miles away.*

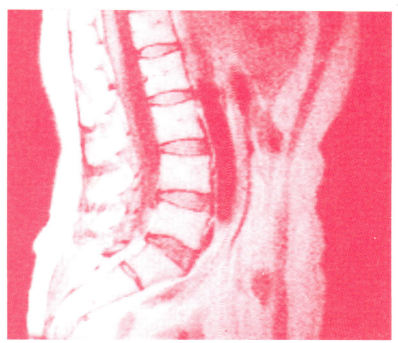

Left: *This photograph was taken using a nuclear magnetic resonance (NMR) scanner. These recently-developed scanners use radio waves to "look" deep inside the body. Here you can see the lower part of a person's back including the spinal cord, bones of the spine, and disks of cartilage between the bones.*

Probably the greatest scientific advances have been made in the field of electronics. Computers were only developed in the 1940s, but today they are all around us and getting smaller all the time—computer scientists have produced a machine that can fit into your pocket and yet do everything that a desk top model can. New ceramic chips have been made, each a few millimeters square, that can hold several silicon chips in a complex arrangement called a "hybrid circuit." Perhaps the most exciting discovery of the last few years is the superconductor, which can carry electricity more efficiently than any other material known.

As modern science advances, new areas for research open up. But new discoveries can lead to new problems. We have not yet discovered a way to dispose of the waste produced by our most recent source of energy—nuclear fuel. This is just one of the problems that present scientists will probably have to leave to the scientists of the future to solve.

Below: *This box shows one of the "superconductors"— substances that can conduct electricity better than anything used so far. To date, only super-conductors that work at very low temperatures have been found, but scientists are working on "hot" ones that can work at normal temperatures.*

SUPERCONDUCTIVITY

Left: A block of copper and a spray of strands of the alloy niobium. Niobium is a superconductor because this fine spray can conduct electricity as well as the whole block of copper. Scientists are now making better and better superconductors that don't have to work at very low temperatures.

Glossary

Acid A chemical substance that will dissolve in water, producing hydrogen IONS. Acids are neutralized by ALKALIS to form SALTS.

Alkali Any of a number of substances which are strong BASES, including soluble metal hydroxides. Alkali metals, sodium and potassium, form caustic alkalis.

Alloy Metal consisting of a mixture of one metal with another metal or non-metal; for example brass is an alloy of copper and zinc.

Alpha Particle One of the three types of RADIATION emitted by some radioactive substances, consisting of two PROTONS and two NEUTRONS.

Alternating current (AC) Electric current that rapidly changes direction from a maximum in one direction through zero to a maximum in the other direction.

AMP Short form of "ampere," the unit used to measure electric current.

Amplitude The maximum value (or maximum height of the waves) of anything that goes back and forth in a cycle; for example alternating current or sound waves.

Anode The positive terminal through which electric current goes into a liquid (called the electrolyte) during ELECTROLYSIS.

Atmosphere The envelope of gases that surrounds the earth (or any other planet, star, or moon).

Atom The smallest part of an ELEMENT that can take part in a chemical reaction. It consists of a positively charged central NUCLEUS surrounded by orbiting ELECTRONS.

Base A substance that reacts with an ACID to form a SALT and water. All ALKALIS are bases.

Beta particles Fast-moving ELECTRONS emitted by some radioactive substances, more penetrating than ALPHA PARTICLES, but less penetrating than gamma rays.

Binary Code A system of numbers that uses only 0s and 1s.

Cathode The negative terminal through which electric current goes into a liquid (called the electrolyte) during ELECTROLYSIS. See ANODE.

Chip A thin slice of semi-conducting material, usually silicon, that contains all the parts that make an electronic circuit.

Colloid A chemical substance with large MOLECULES which disperse in liquid to form a solution that has different properties from a true SOLUTION. Gelatine, starch, and plastics are examples of colloids.

Combustion (burning) A chemical reaction that occurs when a substance combines with oxygen and produces light, heat, and flames.

Compound A chemical substance that contains two or more ELEMENTS combined together, for example salt consists of sodium and chlorine.

Concave Curved inward. A concave lens is thicker at the edges than in the middle.

Condensation The liquid formed when a vapor or gas is cooled.

Conduction The process of passing heat from MOLECULE to molecule that allows heat to be transferred from one part of a substance to another.

Conductor A substance, such as copper, that will allow electricity to flow along it.

Convection The movement of heat from place to place in a flowing liquid or gas.

Convex curved outward. A convex lens is thinner at the edges than in the middle.

Crystal A solid substance that has a definite, symmetrical shape that is formed by the arrangement of its ATOMS and MOLECULES.

Current Electricity The movement of ELECTRONS along a CONDUCTOR that produces a flow of electricity.

Density How heavy a substance is for its size. It is calculated by dividing the MASS of a thing by its volume.

Direct Current (DC) Electric current that always flows in the same direction.

Distillation A way of separating or purifying liquids by heating them until they boil and condensing the vapor produced back into a liquid.

Electrolysis Passing electricity between two terminals (electrodes), through a liquid that contains IONS, in order to produce a chemical change at the terminals.

Electromagnetic Waves Waves of energy that include a range of different wavelengths from short cosmic rays to long radio waves.

Electron A negatively charged particle that orbits around the NUCLEUS of an ATOM. A flow of electrons is an electric current.

Element A substance made up of just one type of ATOM.

Evaporation The way in which liquid turns into vapor as fast-moving molecules escape at the surface of the liquid.

Fission The splitting of atoms and the releasing of large amounts of energy that takes place in nuclear reactors or atomic bombs.

Frequency The number of waves or cycles that occur in one second. A frequency of one hertz is one cycle per second. Frequency of sound waves determines their pitch; frequency of light waves determines their color.

Friction The force that holds back two surfaces that are sliding across one another.

Gravity The force which pulls all objects down to the surface of the earth (or any other planet or moon).

Half-life The time it takes for the RADIOACTIVITY of a substance to decrease to half its original value.

Hertz The unit used to measure frequency, equal to one cycle per second.

Inertia The property of an object that makes it stay still, or resist stopping if it is already moving.

Insulator Either a substance that will not allow heat to pass through it, or one that will not allow electricity to pass through it.

Ion An ATOM that has an electrical charge because it has lost or gained ELECTRONS.

Isotope A form of an ELEMENT that has a different number of NEUTRONS in the nuclei of its atoms from the "usual" form. This gives it different properties, for example whether or not it is radioactive.

Kinetic Energy The energy an object has because it is moving.

Magnetic Field The area around the POLES of a magnet, in which the magnet can exert a force.

Mass The amount of matter in an object. (On earth the mass of an object is the same as its weight. On the moon, the object will have the same mass as on earth but a lower weight because of the weaker pull of the moon's gravity).

Molecule The smallest amount of a substance that can exist on its own.

Neutron An uncharged atomic particle found in the nuclei of all ATOMS, except those of hydrogen.

Nucleus The positively charged center of an ATOM. It is made of one or more PROTONS and, except in the case of hydrogen, one or more NEUTRONS.

Oxidation Making a substance combine with oxygen.

Pitch The quality of a musical sound that depends on the FREQUENCY of the vibrations which produce it. A note of high pitch has a high frequency, while a note of low pitch has a low frequency.

Pole one of the two ends of a magnet at which the magnetic forces are strongest.

Potential Energy The store of energy an object has because of its position. It can be converted to KINETIC energy if the object begins to move.

Primary colors One of the three colors (red, green, and blue) of light that, when mixed, can give light of any other color; OR one of the three colors of pigment or paint (red, blue, and yellow) that can be mixed to give paint of any color, except white.

Proton positively charged atomic particle found in the NUCLEUS of all ATOMS. The number of protons in the atom gives a substance its atomic number.

Radiation (heat) The transfer of heat in the form of ELECTROMAGNETIC waves.

Radioactive Unstable ELEMENTS whose NUCLEI split to emit ALPHA, BETA, and gamma rays.

RAM (**r**andom **a**ccess **m**emory) the part of a computer's memory in which programs and data are held temporarily. Programs and data in the RAM can be changed by the person using the computer.

Reflection The bouncing back of a sound or light wave as it hits a surface.

Refraction The bending of a ray of light as it passes from one substance to another, for example, from glass to air.

Resistance The way in which an electrical circuit opposes the flow of electric current through it. Resistance is measured in ohms and is equal to the voltage divided by the current.

ROM (**r**ead **o**nly **m**emory) the part of a computer's memory that has its program permanently fixed, usually by the manufacturer. Users cannot program the computer to change this memory.

Salt The chemical substance formed when a BASE reacts with an ACID. Common salt is sodium chloride.

Solution A liquid that contains a solid (or gaseous) substance completely dissolved in it.

Static Electricity Non-moving electric charge on an object, often produced by friction, for example, rubbing an object with fur.

Transistor A semi-conducting electronic component that can amplify signals or turn AC into DC.

Vacuum A space in which there are no ATOMS or MOLECULES. (Perfect vacuums are impossible to make so "vacuum" usually means a place where the pressure is much lower than normal air pressure.)

Volt The unit used to measure electrical pressure.

Wavelength the distance between the peak of one wave and the peak of the next.

Index

Page numbers in *Italic*
refer to pictures.

Photographic Acknowledgments

Front cover: ZEFA; page 2 John Walsh/Science Photo Library; 10 ZEFA; 18 Dr Jeremy Burgess/Science Photo Library; 19 ZEFA; 20 North of Scotland Hydro-Electric Board; 27 ZEFA; 29 Courtesy, THORN-EMI top, ZEFA bottom; 35 TRH Pictures; 36 Aspect Picture Library; 37 David Scharf/Science Photo Library; 39 ZEFA; 40 Charles Falco/Science Photo Library; 42 Williams & Metcalf/Science Photo Library; 43 Will McIntyre/Science Photo Library; 49 Courtesy, Ferranti plc top, Dick Luria/Science Photo Library bottom; 52 ZEFA; 53 Lucasfilm/Kobal Collection left, UFA/Kobal Collection right; 54 ZEFA; 57 ZEFA; 61 Paul Brierley; 65 TRH Pictures; 67 Central Electricity Generating Board; 70 Derby Museum & Art Gallery; 72 Ed Barber/The Conservation Unit, Museums and Galleries Commission; 73, 75, 78, 80 ZEFA; 81 Geological Museum, London top and middle right, Geoscience Features Picture Library bottom right; 82 Swift Picture Library top, Greenpeace bottom, Robert Harding Picture Library bottom inset; 86 Martin Dohrn/Science Photo Library; 91 Central Electricity Generating Board; 93 ZEFA; 97 ZEFA left and right; 99 P & G Bowater top, Shell International Petroleum Company middle and bottom; 105 Courtesy, Courtaulds; 106 Design Council; 109 ZEFA left, courtesy Lockheed right; 110 and 111 Pilkington Glass; 115 Rank Xerox; 117 ZEFA; 118 All-Sport top, Robert Harding Picture Library bottom; 119 University Hospital and Medical School, Nottingham top, Paul Brierley bottom.

Picture Research Sarah Donald

ABE-5979